# Humble Boy

Charlotte Jones' first play, *Airswimming*, was premièred at the Battersea Arts Centre, London and later broadcast on Radio 4. *In Flame* was premièred in January 1999 at the Bush Theatre, London, and revived at the New Ambassadors, London, in September 2000. *Martha, Josie and the Chinese Elvis* premièred at the Bolton Octagon in April 1999 and transferred to the Liverpool Everyman in May of that year. It won the *Manchester Evening News* Best Play Award and the Pearson Television Best Play Award of 1999. It was recently revived at the Watford Palace Theatre. Charlotte Jones won the Critics' Circle Award for Most Promising Playwright in 2000 for *In Flame* and *Martha, Josie and the Chinese Elvis*. *Humble Boy* was awarded the Susan Smith Blackburn Award, 2001, the Critics' Circle Best New Play Award, 2002, and the People's Choice Best New Play Award, 2002.

# CHARLOTTE JONES

# Humble Boy

Faber and Faber

New York / London

Faber and Faber, Inc.
An affiliate of Farrar, Straus and Giroux
19 Union Square West, New York 10003

Faber and Faber Ltd
3 Queen Square
London WC1N 3AU

Library of Congress Control Number: 2003103677
ISBN: 0-571-21287-5

1   3   5   7   9   10   8   6   4   2

For my parents

*Humble Boy* was commissioned by Anna Mackmin and Matthew Byam Shaw. It had its world premiere at the Royal National Theatre, London, in August 2001 before transferring to the West End under Matthew Byam Shaw and Act Productions Ltd in January 2002.

*Humble Boy* had its U.S. premiere at the Manhattan Theatre Club in New York City in May 2003; Lynne Meadow, artistic director, and Barry Grove, executive producer. *Humble Boy* was directed by John Caird; sets and costumes were designed by Tim Hatley; lights were by Paul Pyant; and sound was by Christopher Shutt. The production stage manager was Roy Harris.

CAST OF CHARACTERS

| | |
|---|---|
| Felix Humble | Jared Harris |
| Mercy Lott | Mary Beth Hurt |
| Flora Humble | Blair Brown |
| Jim | Bernie McInerey |
| George Pye | Paul Hecht |
| Rosie Pye | Ana Reeder |

**Humble Boy,** presented in association with Matthew Byam Shaw and Anna Mackmin, was first performed on the Cottesloe stage of the Royal National Theatre on 9 August 2001, with the following cast:

**Felix Humble** Simon Russell Beale
**Mercy Lott** Marcia Warren
**Flora Humble** Diana Rigg
**Jim** William Gaunt
**George Pye** Denis Quilley
**Rosie Pye** Cathryn Bradshaw

*Music played live by* Charlotte Bradburn (*saxophone*), Adam Caird (*piano*), Zoe Martlew (*cello*)

*Director* John Caird
*Designer* Tim Hatley
*Associate Costume Designer* Lucy Roberts
*Lighting Designer* Paul Pyant
*Music* Joe Cutler
*Sound Designer* Christopher Shutt
*Company Voice Work* Patsy Rodenburg

*The Royal National Theatre production of this play was recorded by the National Video Archive of Performance at the Theatre Museum.*

# Characters

*in order of appearance*

**Felix Humble** *[handwritten: Hamlet] 35 [handwritten: likes George]*

**Mercy Lott** *[handwritten: Polonius late 50s] [handwritten: took care of Felix as baby]*

**Flora Humble** *[handwritten: late 50s] [handwritten: Felix's mother]*

**Jim** *[handwritten: 60s]*
the gardener

**George Pye** *[handwritten: Claudius 60] [handwritten: affair w/ Flora]*

**Rosie Pye** *[handwritten: early 30s] [handwritten: once, lover of Felix]*

*[handwritten: Ophelia]*
*[handwritten: George's daughter]*

*[handwritten: James — Felix's dead father]*

*[handwritten: Felicity (?)]*
*[handwritten: Felix & Rosie's child]*

# Act One

## SCENE ONE

*Set: a pretty country garden. Perhaps the suggestions of a house or a glass conservatory from which the characters enter into the garden. A patio area, perhaps with a path through the garden. At the back there is an area for gardening tools; a gardening chair or stool. There is a garden hosepipe wound up there. Something of a lawn with borders. A rose bush. At the end of the garden there is a large beehive. The suggestion of an apple tree – perhaps just some overhanging branches with a few apples.*

*The stage is in darkness. There is music. Perhaps resonant of 'The Flight of the Bumblebee'. The beehive lights up to suggest the bees leaving the hive. The lights fade up on the rest of the garden. The music is still playing and the hive continues to throb with light.*

*Felix Humble walks in a stumbling, uncertain way into the garden. He is transfixed by the hive. He is an overweight but not unattractive man of about thirty-five. He wears old and slightly greying cricket whites, despite the fact that he is not a sportsman by any stretch of the imagination. He climbs up the steps and takes off the lid of the hive and looks in. The music ends.*

*Mercy Lott enters the garden. She is wearing black clothes with brown shoes. She is in her late fifties, a petite and timid, mousy woman. She watches Felix with concern. She approaches him but doesn't get too close. Felix glances at her, then returns his attention to the hive.*

**Felix** (*he stumbles on the letter 'b'*) The b–b–b–bees have gone.

**Mercy** Yes, dear. Will you come in now?

**Felix** They took the b–bees away. I saw them.

**Mercy** Your mother isn't cross. She just wants you to come in.

**Felix** There were four of them. The bee-keepers. All in white.

**Mercy** I'm sure if you just say a little sorry to her –

**Felix** They looked like astronauts.

**Mercy** Did they?

**Felix** Or cosmonauts. Depending.

**Mercy** On what, dear?

**Felix** If we were in Russia.

**Mercy** Is it still called Russia? Russia?

**Felix** What?

**Mercy** Russia? Is it still called Russia? I can't keep track. Anyway, your mother's waiting inside for you.

*Felix puts the lid back on and climbs slowly and awkwardly down.*

**Felix** What do you call a group of b–bee-keepers, Mercy?

**Mercy** Is this a joke? I'm not very good with jokes, dear.

**Felix** No, I mean what's the word? Like a flock of sheep, a herd of cows, a pack of dogs, a – an exaltation of larks.

**Mercy** Is it really? An exaltation. How lovely.

**Felix** What is it for b–bee-keepers?

**Mercy** Do you know? I've no idea.

**Felix** What is it for astronauts? A group of astronauts?

**Mercy** Shall we discuss it inside, dear?

**Felix** Something to do with them being white. And weightless. And silent.

**Mercy** We shouldn't leave your mother on her own with all the others.

**Felix** I just have to find the right word.

**Mercy** We really should support your mother.

**Felix** (*a flash*) I can't go in until I've found the right words. Come on. A swarm of b–bees. A what of b–bee-keepers? A what of astronauts? A what? There must be a word for it. The word must exist. I just need to get this – just . . . think logically. There were four of them. They were dressed in white – they took the bees away.

**Mercy** A heavenly host?

**Felix** What?

**Mercy** A heavenly host! A heavenly host of bee-keepers, stroke astronauts. I like it. (*Mercy glances anxiously towards the house. She sees Flora approaching.*) Please let's go in now.

**Felix** Or an apocalypse. An apocalypse of bee-keepers.

**Mercy** Lovely. Even better. That's settled. In we go then.

*Flora enters. She is a very attractive woman in her late fifties. She looks young for her age. She wears a stylish navy blue dress and Jackie Onassis glasses.*

**Mercy** Flora! We were just coming in. Weren't we, Felix? We were just sorting out what you call a group of bee-keepers and then we were right with you. Do you need me to do more sandwiches? She's not angry. You're not angry, are you, Flora?

3

**Flora** No.

**Mercy** There. I told you she wasn't angry. We can all go in now. Your mother isn't angry with you.

**Felix** Yes she is.

**Flora** (*calmly*) I am not angry, Felix. I am incandescent with rage.

**Mercy** Oh dear.

**Felix** (*stammering badly*) An apocalpse of b–b–b–b–bee-keepers. What do you think of that for a collective noun, Mother? It's not b–b–bad, is it?

**Flora** Stop that, Felix. You haven't done that since you were at prep school.

**Mercy** He's just a little jittery.

**Flora** He's doing it to annoy me.

**Mercy** I'm sure he's not – you're not, are you, Felix?

**Flora** He can speak perfectly well, if he wants to. He's doing it on purpose.

**Felix** (*extreme frustration*) I'm trying to b–b–b–b–b–

**Mercy** (*supplying the word for him*) Behave? He's trying to behave, Flora.

**Flora** (*coolly*) I'm afraid, Felix, you will not get the sympathy vote. Today your father has a prior claim.

**Felix** I saw them, Mother. The apocalypse of b–b–b– (*He gives up.*) They were here. While my father was being consigned to dust. You got rid of them immediately. His be– his be– be–

**Flora** I got rid of the bees on professional advice. They were swarming. Since your father's death they have developed very alarming tendencies.

**Felix** P–perhaps they were angry.

**Mercy** Felix.

**Felix** I came home and I went through the house and I find all my father's be–be–be– all his things gone. All his clothes.

**Mercy** Flora very kindly gave them to me. For the Romanian orphans.

**Flora** His bee-keeping suit is still there. In the garage. It is a constant reminder.

**Mercy** I could have taken it but Jean who runs the shop was worried there wouldn't be much call.

**Felix** I come home – and there is just an absence.

**Flora** Don't question what I do, Felix. You weren't here.

**Felix** I'm trying to find the right words.

**Flora** Oh yes, Felix, you carry on. That is what this day has been lacking. Yes. There we all were, waiting in the church for you to find just the right words. Waiting for my clever son, my golden boy, the Cambridge don, to deliver his father's oration.

**Felix** I'm not a don.

**Flora** There we all were, thinking he will make this bloody bloody awful thing . . . better – oh, we will cry but we will be uplifted. But instead you, let me find the exact word now, you absconded.

**Felix** I'm not well.

**Flora** Buggered off.

**Felix** I have p–pills.

**Flora** And so it falls to an amateur entomologist, an insect man, not even a close friend, a passing acquaintance of your father's, to find the right words. The *bon mot*.

**Mercy**  He did very well, considering.

**Flora**  He did not do well, Mercy. He compared my husband's career to the life cycle of an aphid.

**Mercy**  I liked the bit about you spinning a web around him.

**Flora**  Oh yes, there was no end to his metaphorical prowess. Men who spend their waking hours studying the mating rituals of arachnids should not be allowed out.

**Felix**  They're his friends.

**Flora**  They *were* his friends. Friends of the *late* James Humble. A group of tedious entomologists. No, no, let me adhere to the linguistic rules that have been imposed on us today. A boredom of entomologists. A woeful irritation of insect men. Open up their collective thorax and you will not find a beating heart among them.

**Mercy**  Shall I go and make some more sandwiches? I thought the beef paste was going down rather well.

**Felix**  I haven't b–b–been well.

**Flora**  Your father is dead, Felix. Your being unwell barely registers on the Richter scale.

**Felix**  I tried to sp–speak – to sum his life up –

**Flora**  We are every one of us unwell. Do not deceive yourself that you hold the monopoly. Mercy's not well. She hasn't been right in years.

**Mercy**  Well, a little arthritis in my back –

**Flora**  And I am recovering from major surgery.

**Mercy**  Oh, she is.

**Felix**  (*quietly*) P–plastic.

**Flora** What did you say?

**Felix** A nose job is not major surgery.

**Mercy** Oh, but her face was black and blue. You should have seen it. Even now if you look under those glasses – ah, the bruising, she looks terrible –

**Flora** Shut up, Mercy.

**Mercy** I only meant –

**Flora** Did you not have a more suitable pair of shoes?

**Mercy** What?

**Flora** I've told you about wearing brown and black together.

**Felix** You're not wearing b–black.

**Flora** Black is too draining. Anyway this is Jean Muir. And I have to say I find it rich, yes, ripe that I am being criticised on my choice of – look at you! Did you seriously think that this was appropriate attire for your father's funeral? You don't even play – you were a horror when it came to ball games. In fact I don't recognise you. Look at yourself. You've grown fat and unkempt. How could you do this?

**Mercy** Should I pop home and change them?

**Flora** Oh please go in, Mercy. See to the insect men. Wreak havoc with some potted shrimp, for Christ's sake.

**Mercy** Right. Yes. Good idea. You'll be all right?

**Flora** Oh yes, yes. My husband is dead and my only son, who has grown fat and strange, has just run away from his own father's funeral. I'll be fine. Fine. At least those bastard bees are gone.

*A moment, then Mercy leaves apologetically.*

**Mercy** Yes. Yes. Sorry, Flora.

*Felix and Flora stand there.*

**Felix** B–b–blessed are the p–p–peacemakers.

**Flora** For they shall irritate the hell out of you . . . I saved up a long time for that operation.

**Felix** I know.

**Flora** Your father wanted me to – (*carefully*) he didn't not want me to – he knew what it meant to me.

**Felix** Yes.

**Flora** I didn't even know he was in the garden. I was upstairs, resting, when he collapsed. I couldn't hear – the bandages covered my ears, muffled the sound. But I knew. I was reading *Vogue* and suddenly it dropped from my hands. Just fell to the floor. But there was nothing – he was dead in an instant, you know, his heart –

**Felix** Yes.

**Flora** I couldn't bear to have his things. I couldn't bear –

**Felix** It doesn't matter.

**Flora** Perhaps I should have kept – for you – but really, you haven't been here in such a long time –

**Felix** Just because you can't see something doesn't mean that it isn't there.

**Flora** (*sharply*) What?

**Felix** B–black holes. They're not observable. Well, without very sophisticated microlensing techniques they're not.

*Pause. Flora is wrong-footed.*

**Flora** Don't try and blind me with science, Felix.

**Felix** I'm not.

**Flora** You made me look like a fool in that church. This is not something that I will be able to forgive, Felix.

**Felix** No.

**Flora** This is not something that I will be able to forget.

**Felix** No.

*She turns to go, turns back.*

**Flora** What pills are you taking?

**Felix** It's nothing. Nothing. For nerves. Just to help me sleep.

**Flora** I always know when you are ill.

**Felix** Yes.

**Flora** Well, you're too old now for me to . . . Are you going back today?

**Felix** I don't know yet.

*She looks at Felix intently. The gardener Jim walks into the garden. He is in his sixties, thoughtful and quiet, even absent-minded, with a gentle sense of humour. Felix stares at him, Flora does not look at him. He carries a hoe and a bucket of ashes and tea leaves. He scatters the ashes under the rose bush, spreads them. Flora looks away, around the garden.*

**Flora** It's such a beautiful day. Shame.

*She walks back into the house, giving the hive a wide berth. Jim glances at her as she leaves. Felix continues to look at Jim. Jim notices him watching.*

**Jim** I know, I know. I thought twice about coming today. But what with this hot weather, it all needs doing and your mother can't bear it getting out of hand, can she?

**Felix**  No, she can't.

**Jim**  (*looking at the roses*) This has definitely come out of itself today . . . (*He dead-heads the bush.*) I like the floribundas but Mrs Humble is fond of the hybrids. They smell sweeter of course. That always swings it for her. I'd go for more variety but she only wants the scented flowers. And I do as I'm told.

**Felix**  Yes.

**Jim**  This one's a hybrid tea, *Rosa 'Josephine Bruce'*. Don't know who she was, Josephine, but she's got quite a jolly flower named after her. Beautiful dark crimson, lovely scent – and so easy. Positively rampant. Makes me think Miss Bruce must have been a bit of a goer in her day.

**Felix**  She might not be dead. Josephine B–b–b–

**Jim**  No, you're right, she could still be at it. But often they are, aren't they? Dead, I mean. And this is a nice way of carrying them on. For their family.

**Felix**  Yes.

**Jim**  You'd be surprised how many are named after the strangest people. There's a pink climber called Bobby Charlton. Not that he's dead. Or is he? Anyway, it's a real blowsy thing, I always wondered if he had a hand in choosing it for himself. I rather hope he did . . . Sorry, listen to me, I'm not thinking. Are you all right, lad?

**Felix**  The b–b–bees are gone.

**Jim**  I know, it's a sad day. Very sad. A hive without its bees. It says it all, doesn't it?

**Felix**  I saw it. There were four of them. An apocalpse. In all their regalia. White with their veils on, carrying their boxes and the – you know – (*He searches for the word.*)

**Jim** Smokers?

**Felix** Yes.

**Jim** To pacify the bees, I know.

**Felix** It was strange. No, it was beautiful.

**Jim** (*smiles*) Was it? (*Jim enjoys the story of the bee-keepers.*)

**Felix** I was watching from upstairs and the sky was black with bees. But the bee-keepers didn't panic.

**Jim** No. They wouldn't.

**Felix** They placed a white sheet on the ground and reached up towards the bees. And what was odd – from where I was upstairs, from that angle, with the blackness of the sky and the whiteness of their suits, it seemed like they lifted right off the ground. It made me – I can't describe it exactly – but it, it made me want to cry.

  *Pause.*

**Jim** Don't tell Mrs Humble, but there's still some left.

**Felix** What?

**Jim** Bees. The ones that got away. They've outwitted her. God love 'em.

**Felix** But the hive is empty.

**Jim** No, not in the hive. *Bombus hortorum*. The garden bumblebee. There's a nest underneath the shed. I found it just the other day. At least they look like *hortorums*.

**Felix** You didn't tell her?

**Jim** If she wants her flowers, she should be thankful for some friendly neighbourhood bees. Anyway, they'll die off soon. They'll only last the summer, not like the honey-bees. I think we should leave them in peace, don't you?

**Felix**  Yes. Till the end of summer. Yes.

**Jim**  Good lad. It can be our little secret.

**Felix**  I'd better get in now.

**Jim**  Yes. There's quite a gathering in there.

**Felix**  They'll want to see me.

*Felix stumbles away, perhaps steadying himself on the hive as he goes. He looks back at Jim.*

**Jim**  Nice talking to you, Felix.

*Felix nods and exits. Jim starts to hoe around the rose plant.*

### SCENE TWO

*A beautiful sunny day in midsummer. The summer solstice. About two weeks after the funeral.*
   *Jim picks up his gardening implements and exits. As he does so, George Pye enters. Jim looks at him but George does not return the glance. George is a beefy, well-built man of about sixty. He has a large portable CD Walkman on and he carries a jug of Pimms or the equivalent. The headphones are very large. Music – Glen Miller's 'In the Mood' – plays quietly. He puts the jug down.*

**George**  (*he shouts towards the house, rather too loud*) Out here, bunny!

*He turns his Walkman up. We hear 'In the Mood' more clearly. He stretches luxuriantly. He pours himself a Pimms, he is already jiggling along to the music. He dances absently around the garden, banging out percussion on the hive. He comes to the rose bush. He tries to pick a rose off the bush. A thorn pricks him.*

Bugger. Bloody bugger it. (*He sucks his finger, then rips the flower from the bush.*) Got you, you swine.

*He places the rose on the hammock. He checks in his pocket, takes out a ring box. He puts it back in his pocket. This gives him a burst of energy. His moves become more exuberant. He is definitely 'in the mood', dancing as if no one were observing him. He starts conducting the plants of the garden, as if he were Glen Miller. He brings some garden furniture out and sets it up, dancing all the while. Flora enters. She looks radiant in cream. She watches George, amused in spite of herself. He spots her.*

**Flora** George. What are you doing?

**George** Bunny!

*He grabs her and swings her into a jive. For a moment they dance well together. But she is reluctant and tries to stop him after a few extravagant moves.*

**Flora** (*laughing*) Stop it, George.

**George** Can't hear you, bun.

**Flora** You great fool! I can't even hear the music.

**George** Don't need to. Just follow me, bunny.

**Flora** What if someone saw us – stop it – what if Felix . . .? Turn, it off.

*He turns it off. Takes it from his waistband. The music stops.*

**George** He's still here, is he?

**Flora** Apparently he intends to stay till the end of summer.

**George** After what he did to you at the funeral. The little shit.

**Flora** He is my – I can't – anyway, he doesn't seem . . . himself.

> *George snorts in response. He pours her a glass of Pimms. Flora sits, rearranges herself, undoes a button to catch more sun. She looks at the CD player.*

**Flora** Is that your new toy?

**George** It's bloody excellent, isn't it? I even wear it when I'm driving.

**Flora** Isn't that illegal?

**George** Bollocks! I'm going hi-tec, bun. Stereo, On-Digital, widescreen, DVD, that's me.

**Flora** No holding you back.

**George** Rosie bought it for me. I tell you, it comes to something when it's your child telling you to turn your music down.

**Flora** I take it she's not a fan of the big band.

**George** Christ no! I love her to bits but she's like her mother. Born without an ounce of swing.

> *Flora laughs. Pause.*

**George** This is good, Flora. Being out here with you.

**Flora** Yes.

**George** I could get used to this. Flora –

**Flora** (*interrupting*) You haven't said anything, George.

**George** Eh?

**Flora** The bruising's completely gone down now.

**George** What?

**Flora** My nose.

**George** (*mock surprise*) Bloody hell!

**Flora** What?

**George** It's magnificent!

**Flora** You hadn't even noticed.

**George** I had. I was just savouring it. It's bloody tremendous. It's positively Roman.

**Flora** It's not Roman. I didn't ask for Roman.

**George** When I say Roman, I mean . . . Neopolitan.

**Flora** Neopolitan?

**George** Yes! The Neopolitan nose is soft, with delicately flared nostrils and a certain very appealing button-mushroom quality. As far as noses go, it's a bloody classic. It's the Lamborghini of noses.

**Flora** Yes, but is it me?

**George** Let me see . . . And the other side. Yes. It's definitely you.

**Flora** I mean, does it suit me?

**George** You're a vision of loveliness.

**Flora** I don't think I like it.

**George** Oh bun! After all that.

**Flora** Oh, I mean the nose is fine. The nose is quite pleasing, but I'm not sure if my face lives up to it. Somehow it makes the rest of me look – tired. I might need a little lift.

> *She pulls her skin back and up. George takes her hand away.*

**George** You look fine to me.

**Flora** Well, you're biased. Hand me my cream before my wrinkles reach the point of no return.

**George** Let me. (*He puts sun-cream on her face.*)

**Flora** Ah yes, anoint me. That's nice.

**George** Oh Flora.

**Flora** Please don't get ardent, George. It's only half past twelve.

**George** You know what I want, damn it. I know it's too soon, but, I mean bloody hell. I've been waiting in the wings for a long time now.

**Flora** I know.

**George** And it doesn't come naturally to me. I'm not a back-seat driver, Flora. It's a terrible shame, a shock about James and everything but you've been worrying about telling him for so long, I think we should just do it. Grab it by the balls. We can wait a few months, but let's not piss about, the sooner the better, bun. Anyway I've already got you the ring.

**Flora** Really?

**George** I'll make you bloody happy. The words 'pig' and 'shit' spring to mind. In a more classy sort of way.

**Flora** You're such a romantic, George.

**George** How do you want me to do it? On bended knee?

**Flora** Please don't, George, you might never get up again.

**George** I'll swing from the ruddy trees if you want. Shout it from the rooftops, thatched or otherwise.

**Flora** This is a small place, George.

**George** I don't give a bishop's bollock what anyone thinks.

**Flora** George!

**George** I mean bloody hell, Flora. It's not as if you were happy with him.

**Flora** Please don't talk about that.

**George** He was dull. You told me he was dull.

**Flora** That was the wrong word to use.

**George** Look, lover, we've both paid our dues and neither of us is getting any younger.

**Flora** I don't need reminding of that.

**George** (*pleadingly*) Bunny, please . . .

**Flora** Show me the ring.

    *He takes the box out. She looks at it.*

**George** It's a black opal. Bloody unusual, apparently. I can change it if you don't like it.

**Flora** Is it old?

**George** Antique.

**Flora** Mm. What sort of ring did Mary have?

**George** I don't remember, it was years ago, some cheap thing, we were completely brassic at the time –

**Flora** I'm not ready for another ring.

**George** It's not Mary's ring. Rosie has that.

**Flora** I don't like the idea of someone having worn it before.

**George** I can change it, get a new one. I knew I should have let you choose. I've got bugger-all taste.

**Flora** A diamond might have been nicer. (*She closes the ring box and hands it back to him.*)

**George** Is this a no?

**Flora** No. I'll have to think.

**George** Is this a provisional yes?

**Flora** We'd have to wait a bit. Till after – till the end of summer.

**George** You're a star.

**Flora** You'd have to make an effort. With Felix. I know he's – but I don't want any more upset. I can't take it.

**George** I like Felix. We just got off on the wrong foot.

**Flora** What about Rosie?

**George** She wants what I want.

**Flora** But after what happened between her and Felix?

**George** Water under the proverbial.

**Flora** I haven't ever spoken to Rosie. Properly, I mean.

**George** Rosie's not a problem. She wants her old dad to be happy. They're both old enough and wise enough –

**Flora** Yes, I suppose so.

**George** We'll have a little party, invite them all.

**Flora** Nothing showy.

**George** No, no, discreet. My middle name.

**Flora** Yes. It's about time we all got civilised.

**George** Absolutely.

**Flora** This is not a yes.

> *George gets the rose he picked earlier and gives it to her.*

**George** It's enough.

*She takes the rose, smiles and smells it. Felix enters the garden. He watches his mother. He is wearing his cricket whites but with an old-fashioned coloured tank top over them.*

**Flora** That's funny.

**George** What?

**Flora** Doesn't smell of anything.

*He takes the flower and smells it.*

**George** 'Course it does.

**Flora** No. It doesn't. (*She goes to the bush, smells the rest of the flowers.*)

**Felix** Mother?

**Flora** Felix! Darling. You made me jump. Come and join us. Felix, you remember George Pye, Rosie's father?

**Felix** Yes. I do.

**George** Felix. I was just offering my condolences. I'm very sorry about your father's –

**Felix** Yes.

**Flora** Thank you, George. (*to Felix*) You're back very early.

**Felix** Half-day closing.

**Flora** On a Monday?

**Felix** Jean is a very whimsical woman.

*She looks at him oddly.*

**Flora** What is that top you're wearing?

**Felix** Perk of the job.

**Flora** It doesn't suit you, darling. Felix has been helping Mercy out at the charity shop. I'm not sure why.

**Felix** Apparently I'm a natural. Jean says I've got a job for life, if I want. I shifted more in two hours than Mercy does in a week.

**George** Oh yes?

**Felix** But then it's for a good cause. The Romanian orphans. And I have a particular affinity with them, being half way to orphan status myself. I like the second-hand nature of it all. Used goods do have a special appeal all of their own, don't they? (*He spots the jug of drink.*) Ah, nectar! It's a scorcher today, isn't it? Of course it's the summer solstice. The longest day. It's all downhill from now on. (*He helps himself to a drink.*)

**Flora** (*a slight edge*) You're very honey-tongued today, Felix . . . But I think you should calm yourself, don't you?

**Felix** Oh I am calm. I am wonderful. And you are looking ravishing, Mother, if I may say so.

**Flora** Thank you.

**Felix** Not even a hint of widow's weeds.

   *Flora laughs.*

**Flora** (*a little forced*) He's only joking.

**Felix** Oh yes, it's all in jest. Now how are you? How is your fleet, George Pye?

**George** What?

**Felix** Pye's Coaches.

**George** Well, I'm semi-retired now. Some other bugger does the dog work for me. I still do the odd Oxford run though, if we're short. I'm not proud. Can't quite hang up the old driving gloves, you see.

**Felix** No, I bet you can't. What was the legend now? 'Travel Pye –' don't tell me – 'travel Pye –'

**George** (*pleased*) '– if you want to fly.' 'Travel Pye if you want to fly.'

**Felix** Ah yes. A fleet of Flying Pyes. Did you come up with that?

**George** I did, as a matter of fact.

**Felix** Genius. Absolutely inspired.

**George** Thank you very much.

**Felix** Only thing is, I remember being rather disappointed the first time I travelled on one of your coaches. It was all curiously earthbound, you see. Not at all P–pye-in-the-sky-ish. But then you weren't driving. Perhaps they needed George himself at the helm to really make them lift off.

**Flora** It's just as well, Felix. You don't really have a head for heights.

**George** When are you going back to your – erm, studies?

**Flora** He hasn't completely decided, have you? A little break will do him good.

**George** Astrology, isn't it?

**Felix** What?

**George** Your bag. Astrology.

**Felix** No.

**Flora** It's like astrology, darling. It's not a million miles away.

**Felix** Theoretical astrophysics. I think the differences between the two could be measured in light years.

**George** It's all the same to me.

**Flora** And me. But he's a clever boy.

**George** Don't believe in it myself, anyway.

**Felix** What?

**George** Horoscopes. A load of balls.

**Felix** Really? I bet you're a Taurean then, aren't you?

**George** (*as if he is getting the joke*) Ah! Yes! Good one.

**Felix** Yes, definitely Taurus, the b–bull. Born in the month of May. When's your birthday, George Pye? When's his b–birthday, Mother?

**Flora** Well, you know, it is May. It is May, isn't it, George? But you could be on the cusp.

**Felix** Bullseye. Perhaps you're right, George Pye. Perhaps astrology is, after all, my b–bag. Here I was thinking that all the other sciences were woolly and descriptive, that there was something p–pure and exact and fundamental about theoretical physics, that it would unveil for me the secrets of the universe but now I see I was mistaken. I should have got myself a sparkly waistcoat and a pair of coloured contact lenses and started b–bandying a few predictions about. At the summer solstice, with the happy conjunction of Venus and Saturn, all Taureans born on the cusp will find themselves going out on a romantic limb.

**Flora** Stop it, Felix.

**George** Look, son –

**Felix** I am not your son. Did you know my father well?

**George** In passing . . . Your father was a very decent man.

**Felix** Decent. Decent? Yes. I'm compiling a list of adjectives, you see. My father's true nature is proving very difficult to pin down. Decent. Upright. Upstanding. Clean-living. Respectable. But not b–brave, no, we wouldn't go as far as b–brave. No, brave doesn't come into it. Just outside the spectrum. Although there is passion there, yes, give him his dues, he was passionate about his bees.

**Flora** Felix. I want you to stop this now. I am asking you nicely.

**George** Don't worry, Flora. I must be on the road.

**Felix** The Egyptians believed the first bee was created from a teardrop of the sun god, Ra. Did you know that, George Pye?

**George** No, I didn't. Thank you for the drink, Flora.

**Felix** The sun cried bees. I like that. One minute it's raining cats and dogs. The next it's shining bees. You could say it about today, couldn't you? It's shining bees. Except technically the bees have gone, banished by my mother. The bee-loud glade is suddenly beeless. Apparently sans bee.

**Flora** I don't know why he's suddenly so attached to the idea of the bees. You used to be more against them than me.

**Felix** No I didn't.

**Flora** You hated the noise, the droning, while you were studying. And you point-blank refused to eat any more honey.

**George** I ought to be going. Just a 'flying visit'.

**Flora** Yes. Yes. I'll see you out, George. I'm sorry about this.

**Felix** Don't forget your flower, Mother. It's already beginning to wilt.

**Flora** Don't push your luck, Felix Humble.

**Felix** I wasn't aware I was lucky, Mother.

*Flora takes the rose and exits. George follows her.*

Fly, Mr Pye, fly.

*George turns round sharply. Flora has gone.*

**George** I don't give a shit if you piss your life away but you keep away from my daughter. You've fucked her life up once already and you're not doing it again.

**Felix** (*quietly*) No.

*George exits. Felix walks upstage. There is a very quiet humming sound. He reacts to it, as if it were tinnitus in his ears.*

Oh no. Please.

*Flora comes back on.*

Ma.

*She sees that George has left his CD player behind. She tuts and picks it up, then sits and puts the headphones on and turns the CD player on. We hear music quietly: Glen Miller's 'Don't Sit under the Apple Tree'. Perhaps she mouths the words to the song. There is a lighting change. It is as though time slows down for a moment. She cannot hear Felix.*

Ma, I keep dreaming that I am at home and I am a baby and you place me on the lawn. Ever so gently you place me down on my tummy. On the lush, green grass. And you are smiling and I am complete. And then suddenly it shifts and I am like I am now. And I lie myself down on the grass on my stomach and it is green and cool and it takes my weight. And I p–place a gun in my mouth.

*suicide*

It stops the kickb–back this way. I know this. And I want
to b–blow my b–brains into a thousand p–particles.
I want to see the green lawn turn red. And I look at you
standing there above me. And you are smiling.

> *Suddenly Flora senses him still near her. She switches
> off the music. The humming continues quietly.*

**Flora** Felix, don't lurk.

**Felix** The grass is so green this year, isn't it, Ma?

**Flora** I'm not speaking to you!     *rejection*

> *Flora takes the CD player off and exits with it. Felix
> is left on his own. Slowly the humming sound builds.
> Now it is as though time is speeding up.*

**Felix** No, please. I can't b–bear it. I can't –

> *He goes upstage to where the hosepipe is snaked.
> He picks it up and slowly he places it round his neck.
> The humming increases to a terrible pitch. He pulls
> the hose tight. He feels what this feels like. Time
> passes.*     *suicide*

### SCENE THREE

*Mid-July.*
> *Jim comes on. He is carrying a tray of seedlings and
> some compost, and a trowel. He proceeds during the
> scene to plant the seedlings in pots. He is whistling
> 'Don't Sit under the Apple Tree'. He looks at Felix. Felix
> sees him. He is embarrassed. The humming stops. Felix
> looses the hose from around his neck.*

**Felix** I'm sorry . . . I was just – I was experimenting . . .

> *Pause.*

I often use a garden hose. As an analogy, I mean.

**Jim** Oh yes?

**Felix** Yes. Yes. With superstring theory there need to be six or seven extra dimensions. We can't see them but it's like with a garden hose. If you stretch it out between two posts in a field and then you walk half a mile away and look back, it just looks like a one-dimensional line.

**Jim** I'll take that off you, shall I? (*Jim takes the hose off him and starts to wind it up again.*)

**Felix** Yes. Yes. But if you look at the hose through binoculars, if you magnify it, a second dimension – one that is in the shape of a circle curled round the hose – becomes visible. So in the same way there could be extra dimensions in space but you can't see them because they're small and curled up, furled around one another. You see?

**Jim** Mmm . . . Well. Knowing my luck, they'll ban them soon anyway.

**Felix** What?

**Jim** Hosepipes. Last time we had a summer like this, by this time in July there was all sorts of rules.

**Felix** Yes.

**Jim** I know lots of people ignore a ban, but I'm not like that. I watched all the plants flounder. And then I go next door but one and they've got a symphony of sprinklers going off. Drowning the plants, they were. I wanted to report them.

**Felix** Garden rage.

**Jim** But then their plants got blight and died anyway. What goes around comes around.

*Pause.*

**Felix** I haven't seen any of the bees yet.

**Jim** The drones will be out and about soon. Buzzing round the queen. Seven or eight of them joining the mile-high club. Then after they've done their bit she flies away with their torn-off genitals still attached to her. That's women's lib for you.

*Felix smiles.*

**Felix** I'd like to see them. Before I go. I'd feel better, I think.

**Jim** You will.

**Felix** I just can't seem to – I can't seem to ask the right questions . . . I need to make a decision about what I should do next.

**Jim** You want to stop asking all the questions.

**Felix** But it's so hard – with my work, I must question everything. I must –

*Jim stops what he's doing. He looks at Felix.*

**Jim** Felix, you know, bumblebees shouldn't be able to fly. Aerodynamically they're too big, their wings are set up all wrong. They don't obey the laws of physics. But they fly anyway.

*Mercy comes out into the garden. She looks around, although she does not address Jim directly.*

**Mercy** Doesn't the garden look lovely?

*Jim looks at Mercy. She smiles but does not look at him.*

**Jim** Thank you.

*Then he works on in the garden unheeded. Felix glances at him from time to time but he is absorbed in his work.*

**Mercy** Such a beautiful day. I can't remember a summer like it. Mind you, I wish it would rain . . . Now I just popped round with those clothes for you. Jean says she doesn't want any money for them. I've put the bag in your room. But you know I don't think the jacket will fit you, dear. Unless you like a very snug fit.

**Felix** It'll be fine, Mercy, thank you.

**Mercy** Because we've just had another suit in. It's a bit worn round the seat region and the lapels are on the wide side, but apart from that –

**Felix** (*a little too sharply*) I don't want another suit. I want the suit you brought me.

**Mercy** Well, you know your own mind. (*absently looking at the garden*) Isn't that African lily marvellous?

**Jim** *Agapanthus umbellatus.*

**Mercy** But then I love all the lilies. White lilies.

**Jim** *Lilium candidum.*

**Mercy** Tiger lilies.

**Jim** *Lilium tigrinum.*

**Mercy** And the sweet peas. I do love sweet peas.

**Jim** *Lathyrus odoratus.*

**Felix** You know all the names.

**Mercy** Yes.

**Jim** I only know the right names for my little world.

**Mercy** Even from here, they smell heavenly, don't they? (*She stands awkwardly for a few moments.*)

**Mercy** So. What are your plans?

**Felix** What do you mean?

**Mercy** Your mother tells me you're not going back till the end of summer?

**Felix** Does she?

**Mercy** Have you fixed on an exact date?

**Felix** No.

**Mercy** Your mother says you're taking pills.

**Felix** Oh.

**Mercy** What are they for?

*Felix doesn't reply.*

**Mercy** Have you stopped taking them?

**Felix** Are you on a retainer?

**Mercy** What?

**Felix** Or do you just enjoy it, doing duties for her, carrying out her little schemes – *ma/flora*

**Mercy** Felix –

**Felix** Of course she won't do anything that might chip her nail polish.

**Mercy** Your mother didn't ask me to do anything for her.

**Felix** Mercy. You are not a convincing liar.

**Mercy** It's only because she cares –

**Felix** How exactly do you fit into the equation, Mercy?

**Mercy** I've known you since you were born. Your mother and I would play with you here in this garden. I'm a very close, personal friend of your mother's.

**Felix** Ah yes. I see. You like to orbit round her?

*Flora =
black hole*

*black
holes*

**Mercy** Yes, no, I don't know.

**Felix** You should be careful. That's the problem with black holes. The gravitational attraction is so strong you can't resist. But they warp you, they pull you out of shape.

**Mercy** Please don't be sharp with me, Felix. I am of a very nervous disposition.

**Felix** I'm sorry.

**Mercy** It's beyond the pale, really it is.

**Felix** I'm sorry, Mercy.

**Mercy** Is it your work? Is everything all right with your studies?

**Felix** Fine.

**Mercy** Are you a professor yet, dear?

**Felix** No. Research fellow.

**Mercy** Really? Isn't that wonderful? And I remember when you failed your eleven-plus. What is it that you're looking for again?

**Felix** What?

**Mercy** In your studies?

**Felix** It's complicated.

**Mercy** Oh! I like hearing all those funny words.

**Felix** I'm working on M-theory – trying to unify the various strands of superstring theory.

**Jim** Go on.

**Mercy** Mmm.

**Felix** At the root of everything we believe, I believe – a billionth of a billionth of a billionth of the size of an atom, so many noughts it would dazzle you, the perfect

Planck length – there is a loop or a filament of energy – what we call a string – which is the fundamental building block of the universe. And these strings are stretched like the strings on a violin and they're vibrating to and fro.

**Mercy** Really?

**Felix** I know they're there – the strings – the superstrings – and they will bring everything together into a perfect elegant supersymmetry – the jittery, frenzied world of quantum mechanics and the gentle curving geometry of gravity. You see we know the rules for the big things like the cosmos and we know the rules for the small things like the atom, but the rules don't agree – it's the superstrings that will bring the forces together. The superstrings will give us a quantum theory of gravity – that's what I want, what we all want . . . You know, I'm so close, I can hear them! I can hear the little vibrating strings inside my head. Even though I can't prove absolutely that they're there, I can hear the patterns they're making, like they're ringing in my ears.

**Jim** The music of the spheres.

**Felix** Mmm. I've just run out of the maths. The equations don't exist for what I can already sense. The excitation modes – the ringing has too many layers I can't – hold all the notes, all the variables, all the harmonies in my head. But one day soon, I hope, I'll have it, M-theory, the mother of all theories, a unified field theory. The theory of everything. And once I've done that – I'll be able to rest.

**Jim** Yes.

**Mercy** Well, isn't that something, Felix? I mean, if you had to research anything, everything would be the thing to research, wouldn't it? If my brain wasn't so puddled, I'd probably be after it too.

**Felix** I'm just waiting for my moment of intuition. My Eureka moment.

**Mercy** I'm sure it will come.

**Jim** It will.

**Felix** Einstein called his moment the happiest thought of his life.

**Jim** You'd better try and have some more happy thoughts then, hadn't you?

*Jim moves further away. Felix smiles as he exits.*

**Mercy** Divine inspiration, that's what you need. Even when I'm arranging the flowers in church I pray for a bit of that.

**Felix** I can already sense what it would feel like.

**Mercy** Can you?

**Felix** I don't mind if it's a quiet moment.

**Mercy** No. Quiet moments can be very agreeable.

**Felix** Stephen Hawking had his breakthrough when he was getting into bed. But because of his motor neurone disease it took him an age. Throwing back the sheets, plugging in the electric blanket, hauling himself up, tucking himself in, required a gargantuan effort. The nerve cells in his spinal cord were disintegrating, his muscles were playing tricks on him, but all the while his brain was buzzing with complex equations. They went showering through him, like Shakespearean sonnets. By the time he set his alarm clock he'd cracked it.

**Mercy** He should have had a duvet. I resisted for a long time, but they're so easy. You just throw them on.

**Felix** Mercy, you are an original.

**Mercy** What a lovely thing to say!

**Felix** It's true.

**Mercy** You'll have your moment, Felix. Probably when you least expect it. Bingo! There it'll be: 'Humble's unified theory of everything.'

**Felix** I have a terrible fear that I will go through life just missing it. Walking past the love of my life.

**Mercy** Well, we've all done that.

**Felix** Have you ever seen an apple fall? Actually fall?

**Mercy** I don't know. I must have done, mustn't I?

*Felix goes over to the apple tree.*
*During this Flora comes out and listens. She carries a gift. Felix and Mercy do not see her.*

**Felix** I've never seen it. I once sat out here, I was ten, I must have just learned about Newton and the force of gravity and I thought I'd watch an apple fall from a tree – I wanted to see that moment – well, what would it be, say, the half second that it takes an apple to drop four metres. I sat out here for eight hours. Nothing. In the end my mother made me go in for my tea. I wasn't even hungry – I nearly choked the food down. I came back out after half an hour and there were three of them on the floor.

**Mercy** Well, Newton just got lucky.

**Felix** And he didn't have my mother.

**Mercy** I'm sure she didn't mean it.

**Flora** On no, it was clearly my fault.

**Mercy** (*jumping*) Flora!

**Flora** You don't know this, Mercy, because you have never been blessed with children, but ultimately everything that goes wrong in your child's life can be laid squarely

33

at your feet. It's what they call chaos theory, isn't it, Felix? I sneezed in public in 1968 and as a result my son found it difficult to connect in social situations for the rest of his life.

**Mercy** He's just shy.

**Flora** I picked up a sweet wrapper that he dropped when he was three and consequently he's a total failure with women.

**Mercy** He went out with Rosie Pye.

**Felix** This is not chaos theory, Mother.

**Flora** Oh well, pardon me for failing in my use of scientific terminology. I didn't have the benefit of your very expensive private education. Mercy, do you mind leaving us for a minute? I want to talk to my son alone.

**Mercy** Of course. (*Mercy exits.*)

**Felix** (*to the exiting Mercy*) End of your commission. Report back for duty later on.

**Flora** Felix –

**Felix** You've got her well-trained, Mother. She's like a very earnest springer spaniel. She flushes the wild fowl off the water so you can come and take a pop at them.

**Flora** She has precious little else to keep her occupied.

**Felix** I hope she gets rewarded.

**Flora** Of course. She gets to bask in my reflected glory . . . You know, paranoia is very unattractive in a man, Felix.

**Felix** What do you expect with my education? I have been taught to apply the uncertainty principle to every p–problem.

*rejection*

**Flora**  Do you know how utterly bored I am by all this science? I have been doubly unlucky in my life. To marry a biologist and give birth to a physicist. Who on earth said God didn't play dice?

**Felix**  Do you want me to go?

**Flora**  If I had been Marie Curie I would have used my bunsen burner to make *crème brûlée*.

**Felix**  Just tell me to go.

**Flora**  I found three more grey hairs this morning. They were not there a week ago.

**Felix**  What do you want me to do about that?

**Flora**  I want you to – you are always welcome, this is your home but I can't bear to see you lolling about out here –

**Felix**  Lolling? Is that what I am doing?

**Flora**  I don't know. I have no idea what you are doing. You never speak to me properly.

**Felix**  You never listen.

**Flora**  Stop it! Stop this! I can't bear it! Your father would have hated this. (*Pause. She touches him lightly.*) Do you remember the first time we took you to prep school? I didn't want to leave you there, you seemed so small, but your father said I had to be strong. And I stood and waved to you while you walked up the long driveway and James was telling me that we ought to go but I didn't stop waving. I wanted you to know that I wouldn't go away that easily. And you got smaller and smaller and further away until you were nothing but a black dot, but I kept on waving. Even when you'd stopped being a black dot, I kept on waving.

*Pause.*

35

**Flora**  (*handing him the gift*) This is for you.

**Felix**  It's not my b–birthday.

**Flora**  No, well. It's not a birthday present.

**Felix**  I don't need presents.

**Flora**  No, well you don't need to need it. That is the appeal of gifts.

**Felix**  What is it?

**Flora**  Why are you always so analytical? Really, you were like this when you were a child. Why don't you open it?

> *He opens it. Flora smiles a little. He takes out a smallish earthenware pot with a lid on it. He is obviously a little baffled by the gift.*

**Felix**  What –?

**Flora**  It's a copy of an ancient honey-pot. Etruscan or Egyptian or something. It's not really to my taste. But your father bought it for me. I thought you would like it.

**Felix**  Thank you. (*Felix smiles a little, he takes off the lid.*)

**Flora**  Careful!

> *He inadvertently spills a little of the contents – a fine powdery ash.*

It's filled quite full.

**Felix**  Oh, Jesus.

**Flora**  What?

**Felix**  Is this what I think it is?

**Flora**  I didn't like the other receptacle they sent them in.

**Felix**  You mean *the urn*?

**Flora**  It was a very ugly, horrible vulgar tinny thing.
I thought a honey-pot would be much more appropriate.

**Felix**  This is him?

**Flora**  The ashes, yes.

**Felix**  Oh, Jesus.

**Flora**  You criticised me for throwing his belongings out.

**Felix**  I just spilled some! I just lost a bit of his nose or
something.

**Flora**  I lost more transferring it to the new pot. I had to
use a funnel.

**Felix**  Jesus Christ.

**Flora**  They got stuck to the sides and I had to rinse them
out.

**Felix**  I don't believe this.

**Flora**  I've thrown the funnel away.

**Felix**  I think you're psychotic.

**Flora**  Oh well, I can't do anything right.

**Felix**  This is my father. You have just handed me my
father in a pot.

**Flora**  Don't be so melodramatic.

**Felix**  You wrapped him up, for God's sake.

**Flora**  I . . . I . . . thought it would make it more formal –
more precious.

**Felix**  You wrapped him up in 'Happy Birthday' paper.

**Flora**  Well, it was all I had to hand . . . I thought this
would help. I thought you could say the words that you

were going to say. I thought that was what was making you so miserable. I thought that we could have a little ceremony. And that then you could scatter him.

**Felix** What's left of him. You tipped half of him down the sink.

**Flora** Of course there's no guarantee that this is your father. These crematorium places are often very slipshod in their arrangements. And let's face it, one man's ashes is . . . another man's ashes.

**Felix** What are you saying?

**Flora** I am saying that your father is gone. I am trying to help you come to terms with this fact.

**Felix** Well, I'm sorry, Mother. I am very sorry that I do not have the same facility as you for letting go –

**Flora** I said my goodbyes at his funeral like any sane person would.

**Felix** You spent nearly forty years of your life with him –

**Flora** You are a selfish, selfish boy. I know what this is about. I know why you couldn't speak about your father. Because you think that you are better than him. What on earth could you have said? He was only a teacher, after all. Head of Biology. And at a girl's school, of all places! Oh, and he dabbled in bees. Some might call it a pathetically small life. What did he ever achieve, compared to you?

**Felix** Mother –

**Flora** So you look down on him and me and this place. It's all too middling for you with your grand ideas and your big life.

**Felix** That's not true.

**Flora** Well, you don't have to say anything. I know what you think. Just scatter the ashes and be on your way. That can be an end to it. Your father's car is out there, I'll give you the keys.

**Felix** I'm not ready to scatter them.

**Flora** Well, give them to me then, and I'll scatter them.

*She tries to grab the ashes off him. There is a small kerfuffle.*

**Felix** Mother, please. Stop it. I'm not ready yet. Just give him b–b–back. Let him b–b–b–be.

**Flora** All right. All right. This is so undignified. And mind my nose. I've just paid hundreds of pounds for it.

*nose job*

*There is the noise of a car horn off. Flora breaks off. She takes a small compact out and checks her appearance.*

**Felix** What are you doing?

**Flora** I'm going out now. I'm leaving you to your own devices.

**Felix** Is it George P–pye?

**Flora** He has been a very good friend to me since James died but he is afraid to even come near the house for fear of encountering you.

**Felix** Don't go.

*She puts lipstick on.*

**Flora** He's taking me out of myself.

**Felix** Stay here with me.

**Flora** Don't begrudge me my little bit of pleasure. At least I'm making an effort.

**Felix** P–please, Ma. Don't.

**Flora** Felix? What is it? Why ever not?

**Felix** I don't like him.

**Flora** No, well, I'm sure the feeling is mutual. After what you did to his daughter.

*The car horn goes off again.*

**Felix** I didn't do anything – it was –

**Flora** Felix. Must you always have the last word? Do you not realise that the last word is my prerogative?

*Felix goes to speak and thinks better of it. Flora smoothes down her dress.*

I'm going to have a lunch party later on in the summer. Just a small group of people. I hope you will be able to come. But if you are going to be in one of your moods then I would rather you didn't. (*She goes to exit. As she does:*) And you should be wearing a hat in this sun.

*She exits. Felix stands. The humming begins again. He looks at the honey-pot. He takes off the lid and stares inside. He looks as though he might be about to scatter it but he thinks better of it. He puts the lid back on and cradles the pot to him. He walks slowly off. The humming ceases.*

### SCENE FOUR

*The stage is empty. An apple falls from the tree just after Felix has exited.*

*Just afterwards a young woman comes into the garden. She is in her early thirties, healthy-looking but quite plain. It is Rosie Pye. She does not pay much attention to her appearance. She looks around the garden. She sees the apple on the floor. She goes and picks it up.*

*She polishes it on her clothes. Then she sits and takes a huge bite out of it. She swings herself on the hammock and continues to eat the apple in a hearty fashion.*

*Felix enters the garden again. He is wearing a sun-hat and still carrying the ashes. He talks to himself and occasionally addresses the pot. Rosie stops swinging and eating and watches him with increasing horror.*

*During this scene the sun starts to set.*

**Felix** (*intoning*) James Humb–ble was a b–b–biologist and a b–b–bee-keeper. And a husb–band, and a father. A b–b–beloved –

**Rosie** It's only a suggestion, but perhaps you should go for fewer 'b's.

*Felix nearly jumps out of his skin, almost drops the pot.*

**Felix** Oh, Jesus God!

**Rosie** (*proffering him the apple*) Do you want a b–b–bite?

**Felix** Rosie. Rosie. Rosie.

**Rosie** Well, that's a start.

**Felix** Yes, I . . . I was hoping, I should have, I meant to, I really wanted – I thought ab–bout coming to see you, I started to write, I wanted to phone . . .

**Rosie** What about e-mail? Did you consider that?

**Felix** I'm sorry.

**Rosie** Can you put the pot down, please? Just for a minute.

*He does so, reluctantly. Rosie goes up to him and slaps him hard across the face.*

There. I've been saving that up for a long time. Yes. We can be friends again now. Here. (*She hands him back the pot.*) Now tell me what's wrong.

**Felix** Rosie –

**Rosie** Oh no. Not that tone of voice, please.

**Felix** But I want to explain.

**Rosie** It's all right, Felix. I fell in love with you, you weren't as in love with me, you tried to be, you failed, you ran away because you weren't emotionally evolved enough to talk to me about it, you threw yourself into work, I didn't wash my hair for five months, blah, blah, blah, you failed to write, I got angry, I got over it. In a nutshell.

**Felix** Right.

**Rosie** I tried therapy but it was shit. Tae kwon do was much better. A short course in the ancient Korean art of hand-and-foot fighting. Worked wonders. I wasn't very precise in my movements but apparently my battle cries were very convincing. Now take that hat off and let me look at you.

*Felix does so.*

That's good.

**Felix** What?

**Rosie** I'm not in love with you any more. I thought I wasn't but I couldn't be sure until I saw you again.

**Felix** It's b–been a long time.

**Rosie** Seven years, five months, fourteen days.

**Felix** Oh God.

**Rosie** I'm joking. I've no idea exactly how long it's been. It's about seven years. My dad told me you were around again. And against all the odds, I got a slight itch.

**Felix** I've got fat.

**Rosie**  Mm.

**Felix**  I don't look good.

**Rosie**  Mmm.

**Felix**  I haven't b–b–been on top of things.

**Rosie**  Since your dad died?

**Felix**  B–b–before, b–b–but worse since.

**Rosie**  What's with the stutter?

**Felix**  It's funny, sometimes I don't have it. Some days it's fine. I used to do it when I was little but then recently it came b–back. I had to p–present a p–paper, ab–bout b–b–b–black holes. I was supposed to do a follow-up about the B–b–b–big B–b–b–b –

**Rosie**  Bang?

**Felix**  Thank you. I never got that far. My father died so I left. I've b–been at home ever since.

  *Pause.*

I don't think I can go b–back.

**Rosie**  You've given up?

**Felix**  Every time I try to – I hear this ringing –

**Rosie**  (*interrupting*) That's great, that is!

**Felix**  What?

**Rosie**  You left me to become the great white hope of theoretical physics and now you're jacking it in. It was really much better for my self-esteem when I knew I'd been chucked in the pursuit of a Nobel Prize.

**Felix**  It's p–percolating my b–brain, Rosie.

**Rosie**  You're just upset about your dad.

**Felix** I wasn't close to him.

**Rosie** Of course you were.

**Felix** For me, it was always my mother. It was always about her. She b–burnt more br–brightly. Eclipsed him.

**Rosie** Mothers have a tendency to do that, Felix.

**Felix** It's like my mother was the big force – gently warping everything around her. And my father was the little force, fizzing away quietly on a microscopic level. But I can't bring them together. I'm trying to understand the extreme conditions that would have brought them together. I mean, I know the geography of it. It was outside the exam halls of the School of B–biology. London University. My father had just finished his Finals and he walked out and my mother was just p–passing. She'd p–paused to light a cigarette. She was on her way to sign up to a modelling agency. He went up to her and asked her if she'd dropped from the sky. She never got to the agency.

**Rosie** That doesn't sound so extreme.

**Felix** But that's not the physics! The physics of what attracted them and what kept them together.

**Rosie** Maybe you are what kept them together.

*Felix looks at her a moment.*

**Felix** (*shaking his head*) There are too many questions. And now all I have is this b–b–bloody p–pot.

**Rosie** What?

**Felix** He's in here.

*Rosie looks confused, then slightly disgusted.*

**Rosie** Oh.

**Felix** Do you want to look?

**Rosie**  Does it smell?

**Felix**  No, of course not.

**Rosie**  Just quickly then.

  *He lifts off the lid for her. She sniffs slightly.*

**Felix**  Don't sniff at him.

**Rosie**  We buried Mum. I prefer that.

**Felix**  I feel strangely attached.

**Rosie**  It's got bits in it.

  *Felix shuts it rapidly.*

**Felix**  No it hasn't.

**Rosie**  I don't think this is healthy, Felix.

**Felix**  I didn't say it was healthy. Did I say it was healthy?

**Rosie**  When my mum died, I could have fallen apart, I really could. But I didn't allow myself to dwell on – the fact of her death. I know it sounds simplistic – but I made myself think about all the happy times we had together – (*She stops herself. Pause.*) It does get easier, Felix. Time doesn't heal, but it accommodates.

**Felix**  I look forward to that, then.

**Rosie**  I'm trying to help you –

**Felix**  It's all right, I'll get myself a book. 'Happy bereavements. How to grieve in twelve easy steps.' I'll be over it in no time.

**Rosie**  Fine, you do that. Good luck. (*She goes to go.*)

**Felix**  No, please, Rosie. You're right. I'm sorry.

  *Pause.*

It's just I – can't remember – a time of being close, you know. I mean feeling close, feeling – like he was my father . . . The only good memory I can think of is watching the Apollo moon-landings with him.

*He stops. She coaxes him further.*

**Rosie** Yes?

**Felix** I was in my astronaut phase.

*Rosie laughs.*

**Felix** I know, I know, but I was only seven . . . It's still so clear – it's four in the morning, the latest I've ever stayed up in my whole life. I can barely keep my eyes open but then it's the countdown and he reaches out and he takes hold of my hand. And it's like a charge passes from him to me, like he super-adrenalates me. I know this is something huge. I'm suddenly wide awake. We don't speak. But I look at him and he's crying. I am seven years old and I can't b–believe it. I can't b–believe my father is crying . . .

*Rosie looks at him and then leans in to him and kisses him on the lips.*

**Felix** What are you doing?

**Rosie** Put him down. (*She takes the pot out of his hand.*)

**Felix** I don't understand.

**Rosie** You need to get out of your head, Felix. (*She kisses him again.*)

**Felix** I really don't think you should be doing this.

**Rosie** It's all right, I'm a nurse.

**Felix** No you're not.

**Rosie** Yes I am. I trained. After you left.

**Felix** Did you?

**Rosie** The world didn't stop turning, Felix.

**Felix** No, of course not.

**Rosie** I'm training to be a midwife now. You get more glory. When's the last time you had sex, Felix?

**Felix** Are you asking that in your professional capacity?

**Rosie** It's been a long time, hasn't it?

**Felix** (*a lie*) No.

**Rosie** I'm not in love with you, you know.

**Felix** Then why are you doing this?

**Rosie** Because I'm not in love with you.

**Felix** That doesn't make sense.

**Rosie** You can't apply logic to everything. Even in your vacuum-packed little world.

**Felix** No.

**Rosie** Take off your tank top.

**Felix** I'm not doing this.

*She takes his top off.*

Get off!

**Rosie** Yes you are.

**Felix** You can't force me.

**Rosie** You'll really enjoy it.

**Felix** I really really won't.

**Rosie** Just lie back and think of the Big Bang.

**Felix** Please. Please. Stop. You're scaring me.

*Rosie stops what she is doing.*

**Rosie** I just wanted, I thought it would take you out of yourself.

**Felix** I know. And you're – beautiful, brilliant, better than me –

**Rosie** At least it's shocked you out of your stutter.

**Felix** I'm sorry.

**Rosie** You were going to name a star after me. You were going to find a new star and call it Rosie's Star.

**Felix** I only work on stars after they've collapsed.

**Rosie** Well, then you could have named a black hole after me. I'm not fussy.

**Felix** 'Rosie's hole.'

**Rosie** Some people would find that curiously appropriate.

**Felix** You have always been absolutely yourself. That is why I loved you.

**Rosie** I should bloody well hope so.

**Felix** Look at me, Rosie. I'm fat, I'm – look at me.

**Rosie** I don't care. Sometimes time stands still. Just for a moment.

*Felix goes up to her and kisses her tentatively.*

**Felix** I loved the way you used to sleep with both your arms flung above your head. I think about that a lot.

**Rosie** Felix. You liked me when I was asleep because I was quiet.

*He kisses her again. It gets awkwardly passionate.*

*Rosie breaks off. She picks up the pot and moves it to a place of safety.*

Sorry, Daddy Humble. If you could look away. (*She walks back in a mock-sexy way towards him.*) Ten. Nine. Eight. Seven. Six. Five. Four. Three. Two. One. (*She straddles him.*) Houston, we have lift off.

*There is the noise of a car pulling up outside.*

Oh, Felix. Take me to the long grass. Please.

**Felix** The long grass?

**Rosie** The long grass.

*He lifts her up suddenly and carries her to the hammock. It is all a bit clumsy and improvised.*

**Rosie** My big brave astronaut.

**Felix** I think I'm out of my depth.

**Rosie** I'll super-adrenalate you.

**Felix** I don't want to take any more clothes off.

**Rosie** I'd forgotten what you tasted like.

**Felix** I don't even know if it's fully operational down there any more.

**Rosie** You taste like fruit.

**Felix** You might not be able to find it. You might need the Hubble Telescope.

**Rosie** Apricots. Yes. Ripe apricots.

*Rosie laughs throatily. Felix stops suddenly.*

**Felix** What's that? What's that?

**Rosie** What?

*The sound of laughter off. Flora and George are arriving back in high spirits.*

**George** (*off; singing*)
A–B–C–D–E–F–G–H
I got a gal in Kalamazoo
Don't wanna boast
But I know she's the toast of Kalamazoo
Years have gone by, my my how she flew
I liked her looks when I carried her books
In Kalamazoozoozoo.

**Flora** (*off, laughing*) George.

**Felix**  Oh God!

**Rosie**  Don't panic.

*They lie quietly in the hammock or run to a place where they cannot be immediately observed. It is quite dark by now. A moment then George lurches into the garden. He is fairly drunk. He does not see them.*

**George**  Bun, bun! Bunny girl. (*He almost stumbles into the hive. He knocks on it.*) Anyone in there? Or have you all buzzed off? (*He is very amused by his joke.*) We got the better of you, you little bastards. Buzz. Buzz. (*He starts to buzz disdainfully, then laughs so asthmatically he has to lie down on the grass.*) Just need a little rest. (*He looks at the sky.*) Bugger me. Look at the size of it. The moon is out for us tonight, bunny girl. Bunny! Come and look at this.

*He starts to sing or whistle the tune to Glen Miller's 'Moonlight Serenade' loudly, while kicking his legs in the air occasionally. Flora enters from upstage. She does not come right into the garden. She is a little tipsy. George lies on the grass and sticks his arms in the air.*

**George**  Do you wanna dance?

**Flora**  George! Be quiet, you'll wake up my thirty-five-year-old. (*She laughs.*)

**George**  Bunny, the sky is falling on me. I require your urgent assistance.

*She giggles, then hushes herself.*

**Flora**  No, no, shushy. I'm making some coffee.

**George**  No coffee. I'm allergic. I need your urgent-lying-down-here assistance.

*Flora giggles.*

**Flora**  I'm not lying down anywhere.

**George**  Why in God's name not?

**Flora**  I'll get wet. I never get wet.

**George**  Oh no, bun. Look it's bone dry, dry as toast here.

**Flora**  Keep the noise down, Georgy.

**George**  Shushy! Georgy is very shushy now.

**Flora**  Come and get your coffee.

*She exits. During the next he staggers to his feet.*

**George**  Don't go, bun . . . Look at that wonderful arse!

*She waggles it for him and then exits.*

Bunny! It's very, very dry. It's a ruddy heatwave. We're in a drought, bunny. I'm dying of thirst. (*He is on his feet, but still a bit wobbly.*) It's a bloody desert out here. Needs irrigating. (*He undoes his trousers and urinates in a zigzag fashion across the lawn.*) This is a very dry bit. You want to talk to the sod who looks after your garden for you, bun. 'S very, very patchy. It's a good job I'm so full of piss. (*He laughs and then he comes across the pot of ashes.*) Who left a bloody pot in the middle of here? Bloody pisspot. (*He urinates a bit on it and then laughs and steps daintily around it. To the pot:*) Excuse me. Much obliged. (*He does his trousers up.*) Bun! I've done this garden a big favour, I can tell you. It's positively lush now.

> *He exits unsteadily. After a pause, Rosie sits up. She does her top up, straightens herself out.*

**Rosie** I hope he's not going to drive.

**Felix** We've got to stop this.

**Rosie** Well, he says he drives better when he's rat-arsed. He says it doesn't matter if you live in the country.

**Felix** No. My mother. And him.

**Rosie** What?

**Felix** She's making a fool of herself. She doesn't know what she's doing. She's b–bereaved.

**Rosie** Are you serious?

**Felix** I know he's your father, but he's taking advantage of her.

**Rosie** You really don't know?

**Felix** What?

**Rosie** This has been going on for years. Everyone knows about it.

**Felix** What?

**Rosie** They've been having an affair for years. Five or six at least. Look, I thought you knew. I'm sorry.

**Felix** But this is terrible.

**Rosie**  Felix, if you're like me, you'll keep out of it. They're old enough to know their own minds.

**Felix**  This is – this is –

**Rosie**  This is not about you. Or me. I'm sorry, I've really got to go.

**Felix**  No, please, Rosie, stay and talk to me. I have to talk to you ab–bout this.

**Rosie**  My mum died a long time ago. My dad injected her with a sixth of a grain of morphine every four hours. She begged him to kill her, but he wouldn't. I don't like your mother, but I want him to be happy. He deserves to be happy.

**Felix**  No, don't leave me, Rosie.

**Rosie**  I have to. I've got to get back for the babysitter.

**Felix**  What? Oh yes. I'm sorry. Your baby! You haven't said anything about your baby.

**Rosie**  I don't remember the conversation ever being steered in the direction of my life.

**Felix**  I'm sorry – I wasn't thinking. Tell me about your . . . baby.

**Rosie**  (*curt*) Well, she's not a baby any more, thank you for asking.

**Felix**  Oh. Right. I'm sorry – I'd forgotten – not forgotten – it had slipped my – I can't imagine you – with a child –

**Rosie**  Thank you.

**Felix**  No, I mean – I don't know what I mean. I'm sorry.

**Rosie**  So you did know about her?

**Felix**  Yes. Yes. My mother told me you'd had a child, not long after –

**Rosie** (*quickly, quietly*) No, not long after.

**Felix** But I was in the middle of, you know – and I should have written to congratulate you – but I didn't know if it was appropriate.

**Rosie** No.

**Felix** How old is she now?

**Rosie** (*slowly, looking at Felix*) She's nearly seven. Her name is Felicity. And yes, she's just like her father.

**Felix** What? What? Rosie? Are you saying . . .?

**Rosie** For someone who is supposed to have a brilliant mind, you really are slow on the uptake, aren't you?

**Felix** But my mother said – she said you'd – she said you were with –

*He trails off. Rosie smiles wryly.*

**Rosie** And Felix always believes everything his mother tells him. (*She goes to go.*) I'll see you around.

**Felix** Wait, Rosie. I need to talk about this. You can't just –

**Rosie** Felix, do your trousers up, eh?

*Rosie exits. Felix stands there. He does his trousers up slowly. The humming starts again but it is more dissonant now. The humming increases in volume.*

**Felix** I can't be her – I'm not a – I don't even have a –

*He lies himself face down on the lawn on his stomach by his father's ashes. He stretches himself out.*
　　*Suddenly a light is shone in his face. He looks up blinkingly. Jim, the gardener walks on. He is holding a torch and a packet of salt. He walks up to Felix lying in the middle of the lawn. The humming starts to recede or become more harmonious.*

**Jim** Hello. (*He shows him the salt.*) I was just looking for slugs.

**Felix** (*indicating himself*) Bingo.

*He holds out a hand and helps him up. Jim shines his torchlight once more round the garden. It is almost black except for the torchlight. He shines the torch on the hive. He lingers for a moment. Then the light snaps off. The humming stops.*

*End of Act One.*

# Act Two

*Late summer.*

*As for the first act, except now the garden is set for a party. There is a large table which has been laid for five people. Flora has gone to quite a lot of effort. During this act the light fades very slowly.*

*Jim is there. He is tidying up round the garden. He sees the pot of ashes on the floor. He absently picks it up and places it on the table. He exits at the same time as Mercy enters. Perhaps he makes way for her.*

*Mercy comes out, carrying a very large bowl of soup, with a ladle. Her shoes are a little too high and she proceeds with extreme caution. She is dressed rather eccentrically for the party and in a state of excitement.*

**Mercy** (*shouts back towards the house*) I can manage! (*She places the soup and ladle on the table. Shouts back:*) Oh it looks heavenly out here, Flora. (*She puts out her hand to check for rain. Shouts back:*) I think it'll hold out, you know. (*She adjusts several settings on the table. Shouts back:*) We're a chair short, Flora. (*She waits for a response. There is no response. She sighs, looks around and sees the gardening chair that Jim sat on earlier. She brings it over to the table. It is considerably shorter than the other chairs.*) That'll do for me.

*Then she tastes the soup. She wrinkles her face, indicating that the soup needs something. She spots the ashes, which are now next to the salt cellar on the table. First of all she adds a little salt. Then she takes the lid off the honey-pot and sees what she thinks is pepper. She takes a sprinkle and adds it to the soup.*

56

*She tastes again. She is still not sure. She adds a bigger handful. She tastes. She is more pleased.*

*George enters. He looks dapper. He carries flowers and a bottle of champagne. He comes up behind Mercy and pinches her bum. Mercy is absolutely delighted. She is obviously infatuated with George.*

**George** There she is, the little corker!

**Mercy** George!

**George** Looks delicious.

**Mercy** Gazpacho. Although I held back on the pimentos. I'm worried it hasn't got enough zing.

**George** Gazpacho! Where did you learn to make that?

**Mercy** Oh, I just followed a –

**George** Don't tell me, Spanish Civil War?

**Mercy** What?

**George** Don't try and fool me. I can see through the innocent act, Mercy Lott. You were out there with Franco, giving it some.

*Mercy giggles, hits him playfully. She revels in this attention.*

**Mercy** (*laughing*) You know I've hardly even been outside the Cotswolds.

**George** Balls! We've got a little red under the bed, haven't we? She's only small but she's at the nub of things. Cuban Missile Crisis. Fall of the Berlin Wall. There she is in the background, waving. Cooee!

**Mercy** You do tickle me, really you do.

**George** Where's the main girl?

**Mercy** Inside making the salad. I did the starter and the pudding. To help Flora out, you know. I've done my fig tart.

**George** Well, bugger me.

*Mercy giggles.*

I hope you're not intent on giving us all the trots.

*Mercy laughs.*

**Mercy** No. Although I say it myself I think it's quite a good one. I added a little twist, marinated the figs in honey and thyme.

**George** I'd better go in to her.

**Mercy** Oh yes, listen to me wittering on.

*He claps his hands together and rubs them gleefully.*

**George** I'm looking forward to this. (*He goes to go.*)

**Mercy** George – don't you think it will rain? I said to Flora that it wouldn't because she's cross, you know, at it not being sunny, but I think it might.

**George** Nothing is going to spoil this day. Where's Little Lord Fauntleroy?

**Mercy** He's getting changed.

**George** So he's going to make an effort, then?

**Mercy** Oh, I think so.

**George** He'd better keep his arse in check, or there'll be hell to pay.

*Flora enters behind them. She looks immaculate.*

**George** My *chérie*, look at you, I could eat you up.

**Mercy** (*a little forced*) Leave some room for my fig tart.

**George** Bunny girl.

*He ignores Mercy, embraces Flora, kisses her hand.*
*Mercy looks away, embarrassed.*

**Mercy** Those black clouds are blowing over now.

**Flora** We're not going to have any upset today. We're going to be civilised. Felix has told me he's going to behave and so will you.

**George** I'm always civilised. (*He hands her the flowers.*)

**Flora** Thank you. (*She smells them. She looks momentarily troubled.*)

**George** What is it?

**Mercy** Shall I put them in a vase for you?

**Flora** Yes. And give Felix a shout, will you?

*Mercy exits.*

I don't know why she thought she was invited.

**George** (*intense, sexual*) Hello, bunny.

*George immediately tries to steal a moment with Flora. She is evasive.*

**Flora** And George, you can go and get the wine out of the fridge. Then once Rosie arrives we'll be more or less there.

**George** What is it?

**Flora** It looks like we've seen the last of summer.

**George** What's wrong, bunny?

**Flora** I just want it all to go well.

**George** It will. This is the beginning of everything for us.

**Flora** Yes. Yes.

*They kiss.*

You will see to the wine though?

**George**  Don't worry. (*He exits singing.*)
Love is in the air, everywhere you look around
Love is in the air, every sight and every sound –

*Flora smiles. She is left on her own. She looks around the garden, shivers slightly. She checks the table, moves a few things that Mercy had rearranged. Then she sees the pot of ashes.*

**Flora**  Oh Felix.

*She is about to move it when Rosie enters and interrupts her. She puts the pot back down.*

**Rosie**  Hello, Mrs Humble.

**Flora**  Rosie. I'm glad you could come. It's a crime we see so little of each other.

*They think about it and then embrace awkwardly. Rosie hands her a bottle of wine.*

**Rosie**  I'm not sure if it's a very nice one.

*Flora looks at the label dubiously.*

**Flora**  Actually I never drink Italian white. It doesn't agree with me. But I'm sure we can find a use for it.

*Rosie smiles knowingly, nods. Their chat is stilted.*

Take a seat. The others will be out in a minute.

*Rosie doesn't sit.*

**Rosie**  The garden looks lovely.

**Flora**  I'm worried it's going to rack and ruin.

**Rosie**  The flowers smell wonderful.

**Flora**  Do they? This summer I don't seem to be able to – How is the nursing?

**Rosie** I'm training to be a midwife now.

**Flora** Your father said. How lovely.

**Rosie** Yes. Although I get sick of the dads. The weeping and overwhelmed fathers. I could do without them.

**Flora** Mmm.

**Rosie** Probably because I had to go through it all on my own.

**Flora** Yes. (*She knows her name very well.*) How is . . .?

**Rosie** Felicity.

**Flora** Oh, yes. I should remember that.

**Rosie** She's tremendous, in a little alien kind of way. At the moment her mission in life is to part her hair in the middle, in a perfect, undeviating straight line. *like Felix*

**Flora** You should have brought her.

**Rosie** I don't think so. I'm still at the protective stage.

    *Pause.*

**Flora** I would have liked to have a daughter. I was convinced mine was going to be a little Jennifer. I knitted ferociously in pink. But it turned out to be a Felix.

**Rosie** Felicity is desperate for a little brother.

**Flora** I only had one viable fallopian tube and that had to be blown through. After Felix was born, I decided to rest on my laurels. It's a funny thing, realising that you are no longer the heroine of your own life.

**Rosie** Mmm.

**Flora** (*awkward*) You must bring her round another day. Let her play in the garden.

    *Rosie looks at her a moment.*

**Rosie**  You didn't tell him that Felicity was his daughter. He didn't know.

**Flora**  (*carefully*) I told him the facts as I knew them. I thought if there was something important to say, that you would say it.

**Rosie**  In your infinite wisdom.

**Flora**  As far as I remember, just after Felix left you seemed to have rather a lot of male friends. In any case we didn't really talk about you.

**Rosie**  No, of course not. It must have been a relief. I didn't cut the mustard, did I? Oh, it doesn't matter. I'm very much of the 'fuck you, Mrs Humble' line of thinking. It just makes all this today a little bit ironic, doesn't it?

> *George re-enters with the chilled wine, followed by Mercy, who has put the flowers in a vase. She places them on the table. George makes a huge fuss of Rosie.*

**Rosie**  Here he is. Romeo himself. Hello, Mercy.

**Mercy**  Hello, dear. Don't you look pretty?

**George**  She's not a looker but she's got character and I love her.

**Rosie**  Thanks for that, Dad.

**Mercy**  How's little Felicity?

**Rosie**  She's a ball of energy.

**George**  (*discreetly to Rosie*) You're feeling okay? About –

**Rosie**  I'm fine.

**George**  That's my girl.

**Rosie**  Let's have some wine.

**George** Yes, let's get this party on the road. (*George starts to pour the wine.*)

**Mercy** Not too much for me.

**Flora** Where's Felix?

**Mercy** Oh, I gave him a shout and he says he's coming. He was just sorting out the post.

**Flora** (*bewildered*) The post?

*George ushers Flora to sit.*

**George** Come on. Let's not worry. He'll be down in a minute, I'm sure.

*Flora and Rosie sit.*

**Rosie** Sit next to me, Mercy.

**Mercy** Oh, thank you, dear.

*George seats himself at the head of the table opposite Flora. The only seat left is the small gardening stool.*

**George** First of all I'd like to propose a toast. Raise your glasses. To Flora and her future happiness.

*As they raise and drink their glasses, Felix enters. He is wearing the suit that Mercy got him from the charity shop. It is far too small for him. His ankles and wrists are very much on display. It is, in fact, one of his father's old suits. When Flora sees him she nearly chokes on her wine. The others react strongly.*

**Felix** Oh, wait for me. I don't want to miss anything. (*He snatches up a glass and raises it. It is empty.*)

**George** (*sotto voce*) Jesus Christ.

**Rosie** (*amused*) I think you ought to review your capsule wardrobe, Felix.

**Mercy** I told you it would be an odd fit.

**Flora** Where did you get that?

**Felix** From the charity shop.

**Mercy** I could take the hems up.

**Flora** (*to Felix*) How could you?

**Mercy** It won't take five minutes.

**George** What is it? Bunny, what's wrong?

*Felix helps himself to a glass of wine.*

**Flora** It's James's suit. He's wearing his dead father's suit.

**Mercy** Oh. Oh, dear.

**Felix** I wanted to be smart for you, Mother.

**Rosie** Come on then, give us a twirl.

**Felix** You can never be overdressed, according to my mother.

**George** Take it off.

**Felix** And also there is a deplorable lack of good, affordable millinery around these days. Isn't that right?

**Flora** Just ignore it, George. It's fine. Fine. We're going to have a pleasant day. I'm not going to get upset. It suits you, Felix. Very grunge, darling. (*She takes a sip of wine.*)

**Felix** What's on the menu?

**Mercy** Gazpacho soup.

**Felix** Yummy.

**Mercy** I've never made it before. I hope it's all right.

*Felix goes and sits on the stool. He barely reaches the table.*

**Flora**  Please find yourself a more suitable chair.

**George**  He's fine.

**Felix**  Oh yes, I'm fine. Suitably low status.

**George**  Come on then.

**Mercy**  Let me serve it up.

**Felix**  (*to Rosie, a little awkward*) How is Felicity?

**Rosie**  Fine. She's at a friend's birthday party.

**George**  Causing havoc, no doubt.

*Mercy gets up and starts to ladle the soup out. She goes round the table.*

**George**  All right, bunny?

**Felix**  Sorry. Point of order. Sorry. Can I just inquire about that? Call me old-fashioned but I'm afraid it troubles me. My mother being referred to, even affectionately, as a rabbit.

**George**  She likes it.

**Flora**  And it's very accurate, Felix.

**Felix**  What?

**Flora**  For a brief and rather enjoyable period in the early sixties, I was a bunny girl.

**George**  Complete with fluffy tail.

**Rosie**  (*under her breath*) That makes sense.

**Felix**  What happened? Did you contract myxomatosis?

**Flora**  No, I married your father and he brought me here to Moreton-in-the-Mud to rot my life away. The world did not begin at your conception, Felix, as troubling as that may seem . . . Did you say something, Rosie?

**Rosie** This looks lovely, Mrs Humble.

**Flora** Mercy made it.

**Rosie** Mmm. I must get the recipe.

**Flora** Of course I was thrillingly thin in those days. Before my son robbed me of my figure.

*Mercy goes to serve Flora.*

Not for me. I won't have any, thank you.

**Mercy** Oh Flora. Please.

**Flora** I'm not really hungry. I don't seem to have much of an appetite these days.

**Felix** You're anosmic.

**Flora** What?

**Mercy** Anaemic?

**Felix** Anosmic.

**Rosie** You mean anorexic.

**Felix** No. Anosmia. No sense of smell. It affects the appetite.

**Flora** What?

**George** She's not fucking anosmic.

**Rosie** Dad.

**Mercy** Perhaps it's because of the nose job.

**Felix** It's not because of the nose job.

**Rosie** You've had a nose job?

**Flora** I haven't had a nose job. I have had my nose slightly rephrased. That is all.

**George** And she's not fucking anosmic. If she was fucking anosmic, I'd be the first to know about it.

**Felix** Thing about George, he can always be called upon for an elegant turn of phrase.

**George** Piss off.

**Mercy** Does anyone want bread with it?

**Felix** You have been anosmic, Mother, since the day my father died.

**Rosie** No thank you, Mercy.

**George** Why don't you take a running jump? Preferably in close proximity to a cliff.

**Flora** George.

**Felix** Do you think that's the best way?

**George** What?

**Felix** No, really, I'm interested. What is the best way to do yourself in, so to speak? More wine, Mother?

*suicide*

*Flora proffers her glass. Felix goes round refilling for everyone.*

**Rosie** Pills. But not paracetomol. They're too slow and they do funny things to your liver.

**Felix** So speaks the nurse.

**Rosie** The worst is drinking sulphuric acid. You burn yourself inside out.

**Mercy** I really don't think we should be talking about this at the table.

**Flora** I'd put my head in a gas oven.

**Felix** Ah. The housewife's choice.

**Flora** Anything is preferable to cleaning it.

**Mercy** I've got an Aga.

**Rosie** It doesn't work any more.

**Mercy** Well. It's a bit temperamental to light.

**Rosie** No, I mean, you can't do it with a gas oven. They changed it so you can't.

**Flora** Killjoys.

**Mercy** I don't think you could do it with an Aga either. No.

**George** (*slowly, considered*) A length of hose. Easy.

**Felix** (*sharp*) What?

**George** Only way to do it. In the car. A length of hose from the exhaust pipe. Wind the window up. A glass of whisky in my hand and Glen Miller on the stereo. I'd have an upbeat number first. 'Chattanooga Choo-Choo' or 'Pennsylvania 6–5000'. Followed by 'Moonlight Serenade'. I'd just drift off. Easy.

**Rosie** Dad!

**George** Christ. I never would, Rosie love. It's a mug's game.

**Felix** A length of hose. Yes.

**Flora** What about you, Felix? What is your preferred method?

**Felix** Well, in an ideal world, I'd like to jump through a black hole.

**George** I'm sure it could be arranged.

**Flora** Why, Felix?

**Felix** Just a whim of mine.

**Flora** Tell me why.

**Felix** Well, I'd find out what it was like inside.

**George** How thrilling.

**Felix** It would be for a theoretical physicist.

**Rosie** Who doesn't get out much.

**Felix** Theoretical physicists don't get out much.

**Rosie** Well, come on then, enlighten us.  *black hole*

**Felix** You get to pass through the event horizon and down into the state of singularity. The point where all mathematical equations break down and you break up into a thousand million particles. I think that would be quite satisfying.

**Rosie** Doesn't sound much fun to me.

**Felix** The beauty of it is you get to carry on. Well, maybe you do.

**Rosie** But it wouldn't be you. It would just be bits of you.

**Felix** It'd be the essence of me. I'd be recycled. The particles of my body would go off and form another universe. It's a kind of immortality.

**Rosie** If it's immortality you want, I think it's easier just to have a baby.

**Flora** Is that what you want, Felix? How very mundane. If you can't make your mark while you're here, what's the point?

**Mercy** Nobody's eating my soup.

**Felix** Do you think my father made his mark?

**Flora** No. Sadly. I think he would probably feel that he hadn't.

**Felix** You know, Mother, one day scientists at NASA pointed the Hubble Telescope at what they thought was an empty speck of the sky and they saw a void teeming with galaxies. They saw clusters of stars billions of years old that they never knew about.

**Flora** (*sharply*) What are you trying to say, Felix?

**George** Yes. If you've got something to say, I think you ought to say it.

**Mercy** Couldn't we save it till after the first course?

**Felix** I rather thought that it was you and my mother who had something to say.

**Mercy** I'll get some bread.

**Flora** Sit down, Mercy. You invited yourself, so you can sit through this.

   *Mercy sits down.*

**Rosie** Felix, why are you being so difficult? You know what they want.

**Mercy** He can't think on an empty stomach.

**Rosie** They want to get married. Big deal. You take everything too much to heart.

**Mercy** You're getting married?

**George** Yes, we are.

**Mercy** (*a little crestfallen*) Oh. How lovely.

**Felix** (*raising his glass*) Yes! Isn't it! Come on, Mercy. Raise your glass for the Humble Pyes! A match made in Moreton!

**George** I don't give a fart for your opinion, sonny.

**Felix** And I'm not talking to you, Pops. Just answer me this, Mother. What do you see in him?

**Mercy** Oh. There's a lot to see in George. He's a very nice man underneath.

**George** Thank you, Mercy.

**Mercy** You're welcome.

**Flora** I do not need your blessing, Felix. But it would be nice.

**Felix** It's a bit late for my blessing, isn't it? My father died two months ago but –

**Flora** At last Felix is up to speed.

**Felix** – but this has been going on for years. The world and his wife are privy to this information.

**Rosie** Leave it, Felix.

**Mercy** I didn't know for ages.

**Felix** How could you do this? How could you do this to my father?

**Rosie** There's no need for all this.

**Flora** James knew about it.

**George** What?

**Flora** I told him about George. I told your father that I loved him but that he wasn't enough. He accepted that fact.

**George** You told James? About me. You've never told me that –

**Flora** It didn't concern you.

**George** I can't believe you didn't tell me.

    *Felix starts to laugh.*

**Felix** Bravo, Mother. What a tactician!

**Flora** Your father was generous to a fault.

**George** (*working it out*) But if he knew – and I didn't know that he knew – and he knew that I didn't know that he knew – that . . . that gave him more power than me.

**Flora** It wasn't a question of power. It was a question of balance.

**George** Well. This doesn't change anything now. It doesn't make any difference to how things are now.

**Felix** Are you sure of that, George?

**Flora** You are desperate to turn this into a tragedy, Felix, but you will not be able to. *like King N,*

**Felix** My father fell down dead in this garden. And you were upstairs waiting for your new nose to recapture your lost youth so that you could go off and shag Biggles here –

**George** Watch it –

**Felix** – and all the while my father was dying. His heart was giving up on him. His heart was bursting.

**Flora** No. That is incorrect. His heart was not bursting. He did not die of a heart attack.

**George** Oh yes, boyo, you just wait for this.

**Felix** (*wrong-footed*) What do you mean?

**Mercy** (*a warning*) Flora.

**Flora** Give me a cigarette, George.

**George** You don't smoke.

**Flora** No, well, I am branching out.

    *George gives her a cigarette and lights it for her.*

**Felix** What is she saying?

**Mercy** Don't, Flora.

**Felix** Jesus! What?

**Flora** No, he's asked for this.

**Felix** What did you do to him? Dear God, did the pair of you – what did you do to him?

**Flora** Not me, darling. Not me and George, although that would have made sense, I grant you. No, it was his bees. James Humble was killed by his beloved bees.

**Mercy** It was a tragedy.

**Flora** No. It was not a tragedy. Sad and pathetic and shockingly stupid, ironic, funny even, yes comical, hilarious, but not a tragedy.

**Felix** I don't –

**Flora** Anaphylactic shock. He was allergic to the bee-sting.

**Felix** Don't be ridiculous. He kept b–bees for years.

**Rosie** You can develop it over time, without knowing.

**Flora** Thank you, Rosie, if we want a little Nurse Pye nugget, we'll ask for it.

**Felix** What are you saying?

**Flora** He knew, but he couldn't give it up. May that be a lesson to you about the dangers of obsessive behaviour.

**Felix** What? I don't b–b–b–believe my –

**Flora** If it's any consolation, the bee died as well. I found your father on the lawn, with the bee close beside him. Neither of them was moving but I squashed the bee underfoot anyway. There is something deeply satisfying about the crunch of a dead bee.

*bees/man*

**Felix** I don't want to hear this –

**Flora** Your father always said to me that, when it was time to go, that there was no debate to be had. He said that bees have a finite number of wingbeats and once they are used up, the bees just fall from the sky. In the same way we have a finite number of heartbeats. I doubt whether he would have been satisfied with his quota. But no doubt the bee had a case for grievance as well . . . So there. (*She stubs out the cigarette.*)

**Felix** Why didn't you tell me?

**Flora** I would rather that he died of a heart attack. I am more comfortable with that version of events.

**Felix** More comfortable?!

**Flora** For his sake. It makes him look less of a fool.

**George** This doesn't change anything.

**Flora** You have said that once already, George.

**George** Your mother and I are still going to be married. Whatever you think.

**Rosie** If it's any consolation, after the wedding, I will be your sister and your daughter will also be your niece. If you weren't fucked up before, this will really send you reeling.

**Flora** Ah, Rosie. Just when the conversation was flagging.

**George** Rosie. Fliss isn't his – you promised me she wasn't –

**Flora** She's not his daughter.

**Mercy** I don't think I can cope. (*Mercy starts to cry silently.*)

74

**George** Rosie – you said it was that long-haired lad from The Bell. You promised me.

**Rosie** She's Felix's daughter.

**Flora** Not without DNA evidence she's not.

**George** You don't know that for sure, do you? Rosie?

**Rosie** I'm her mother and I know.

**Flora** I'm not a grandmother. She's lying –

**Rosie** I'm not.

**George** But there's no proof, is there, love?

**Flora** Of course there isn't.

**Felix** (*desperate*) Rosie. I have been walking around with this for four weeks. I have b–been trying to rise to this. I have been trying to feel what this feels like. Please don't lie to me.

**Rosie** I'm not lying. After you left, I . . . I did sleep with a few men –

**Flora** I'm sorry. Forgive me for being pedantic but 'a few' is not the correct collective noun in this case.

**Rosie** Dad, tell her.

**George** You did put yourself about, Rosie love.

**Rosie** I was heartbroken at the time.

 *Felix stands up.*

**Felix** I'm sorry. This is too much.

**Flora** Sit down. You will not walk out on me again. I deserve more respect from you.

**Felix** Why?

**Flora** Because I am your mother.

**Felix** You have to do a bit of mothering in order to earn that title. And sadly that has never been your strong suit, has it?

**Flora** What?

**Felix** You don't love me, Mother.

**George** Oh, Christ on a bike.

*George takes out his headphones and puts them on during the next.*

**Flora** Of course I do. You are my son.

**Felix** That doesn't follow. You know that.

**Flora** You're talking nonsense.

**Felix** I am sure you tried. But you couldn't do it.

**Rosie** Love embarrasses you, Felix. You can't turn it into an equation. There is no constant as far as you are concerned. Dad. Take them off.

**George** I'm not listening to his crap.

*He turns the music up. He taps away to it.*

**Mercy** There is no point in being constant in love. It's seen as a sign of weakness.

**Flora** (*to Mercy*) Oh God! I don't know why you're crying.

**Mercy** I may as well throw the soup away.

**Flora** None of this has anything to do with you.

**Rosie** Oh Mercy, don't cry. It's all right.

**Flora** Take those bloody headphones off right now, George, before I rip them off.

**George** (*he can't hear*) What? (*He takes them off.*)

**Rosie** (*to George*) Mercy's upset.

**Mercy** (*crying*) I'm sorry, sorry, sorry. I get these brief bursts of unutterable sadness. I'm taking a herbal remedy.

**Rosie** Are you?

**Mercy** Yes. It's for people who soldier on in the face of complete hopelessness, but it hasn't made any difference –

**George** You've got nothing to cry about, little Mercy.

**Flora** Of course she has. She has never been married, she has no dress sense to speak of and she has always been in love with you, George.

**Rosie** You're a bitch.

**Mercy** (*to Flora*) What?

**Flora** It's true, Mercy.

**Mercy** (*terribly embarrassed*) No! No! No. I have not – I like George, but I have never really – you are very rude to me, Flora.

**Rosie** She thinks she's too good for all of us.

**Mercy** And if you four are anything to go by I'm very glad I've kept myself to myself, thank you very much.

**George** Absolutely.

**Mercy** It's people like you that give people who live in the countryside a bad name.

**George** Hear, hear.

**Mercy** I know that I am a negligible sort of person. But I won't stand for it. I've always looked up to you. Always.

**Flora** You have no life of your own so you constantly leech off mine.

**George** Flora, stop it.          *cruelty of Flora*

**Flora** I did not choose you to be my friend. It was an accident of geography. Because I am stuck in this bloody awful middle-England middle-class bloody rural bloody idyll.

**Felix** (*with sudden authority*) Stop it, Mother. ENOUGH! That is enough now. You have said enough. We have all said enough. It's a beautiful day and . . . and I think we should eat now. Whatever our differences – I think we should eat.

    *Pause.*

Perhaps you'd like to say grace for us, Mercy. Then we can eat your delicious soup.

**Mercy** I don't know.

**Felix** Please. We are all going to be calm now. We have exhausted ourselves. See.

    *Everyone is quiet round the table.*

**Mercy** Very well. (*Mercy goes to stand up. She cannot quite look George in the eye.*) I don't have those sort of feelings for you, George.

**George** No, of course not.

**Mercy** So long as you know that.

**George** I know that.

    *She stands up a little shakily. They all bow their heads, except perhaps Flora.*

**Mercy** For what we are about to receive, which none of you really want to eat but which I stayed up till two in the morning to make and I didn't even have any pimentos and had to improvise round them, may the Lord, whether you believe in Him or not, I know you don't, Felix, because you're a scientist so you're not allowed to and anyway I don't know if I do, because of things like James dying in the way that he did and little Felicity not having an identifiable father and the terrible things that Flora has said to me and the little fat bumblebees just dropping down dead from the sky. And I know that what James said about the finite number of heartbeats should be a comfort, but it is not. And maybe I don't have much of a life but up to now God has filled all the gaps but now there do seem to be holes that He can't fill so perhaps you are right, Flora, because even though I still do the flowers in church and my various parish duties really I would say that I was unofficially on a sabbatical from God at the moment because everything is really so unsettling and I'm sick to my heart of trying all the time, trying, trying, trying, and I don't like it, I don't like it at all so may the Lord, even though we're not on speaking terms, make us all, and I mean all of us, truly grateful. Amen.

**George** Amen.

**Felix** Very well put, Mercy.

**George** Let's eat. I'm starving. (*He takes a mouthful.*) It's bloody delicious.

**Rosie** It's got a real zing to it.

**Mercy** There isn't too much seasoning?

**Felix** No. It's just right.

*They all eat, making some noises of satisfaction and reassurance for Mercy. Suddenly Flora stops, puts her spoon down.*

**Flora** One minute.

**Felix** (*a warning*) Mother?

**Flora** I would really rather prefer it if Felix took his father off the table.

*Felix takes the urn off the table. He holds it to him. Mercy watches him.*

**Mercy** That's –

**Flora** The remains, yes. He insists that he is not ready to scatter them but I think we can do without them at meal-times. Thank you, Felix.

**Mercy** No! No! No! Don't eat it! Stop! Don't eat it. I'm sorry.

**George** What's the matter, Merc?

**Mercy** No, please. I forgot a vital ingredient. I did something inadvertent. (*She's grabbing the plates off everyone and pouring the soup back into the tureen.*) It's contaminated. It's dangerous. I'm sorry. Give it back to me at once.

**Flora** I thought you were dying for us to eat it.

**Mercy** No, no, no, I'm not. I'm leaving now. This is a very bad day.

**Rosie** It's lovely, Mercy.

**Mercy** Oh no. No. No. No. Please excuse me. Ignore me. Chat among yourselves. I have to – urgently attend to the fig tart. (*Mercy grabs the tureen and exits.*)

**George** I think she's flipped her lid.

**Flora** You took her part against me.

**George** No I didn't. I feel a bit sorry for her, that's all.

**Flora** Well, some people are just unfortunate, it's not my fault.

**Felix** Mother, go and apologise to her.

**Flora** What?

**Felix** Say sorry to her.

**Flora** I will not.

**Felix** She is lonely and she thinks the world of you. Tell her that you didn't mean it. You'll feel terrible tomorrow if you don't.

*Pause. Flora gets up.*

**George** Do you want me to come?

**Flora** No, I do not. In any case it won't take long.

*Flora exits. The other three are left. George is quite drunk by now. Rosie sits quietly and Felix holds his dead father's ashes.*

**Rosie** Well, it's all going very well so far.

*George stares at Felix.*

**George** What does he look like?

**Rosie** Dad.

**George** Winnie the bloody Pooh! Here, Winnie, I'm going to marry your mother, whatever you –

**Rosie** Dad. Let's change the subject. Talk about something different. There must be something that we can talk about calmly.

*Pause that stretches towards a silence.*

I know the range of possible topics is fairly limited. But come on. Let's have someone's starter for ten.

**Felix** Glen Miller took a long time to find his sound, didn't he?

**George** Yes.

*Pause.*

**Rosie**  Okay. Another go.

*Pause.*

**George**  Do you know why I called my coach firm the Flying Pyes?

**Rosie**  What you going on about, Dad?

**George**  No, no, Rosie. It's kosher. He wanted to know this. He asked me.

**Felix**  I did, after a fashion.

**George**  See, Rosie, love, just a friendly little chit-chat. Go on then, ask me.

**Felix**  Why did you call your coach firm the Flying Pyes?

**George**  For my dad. (*casually*) He was RAF, flew in the war. Lancasters, Halifaxes, Stirlings. He said the noise of the engines was unbearable – a droning so terrible and the planes were unpressurised and cold, twenty degrees below zero, Fahrenheit that is, so cold you couldn't think. He had to piss into a funnel, the desert lily they called it. They gave them all a survival kit with Horlicks tablets and a Mae West flotation jacket.

**Felix**  Really?

**George**  Yes, really. See, Rosie, it's all going nicely. We're getting on like a house on fire. May I continue?

**Rosie**  Go ahead.

**George**  He went on thirty sorties, he flew with two engines gone, he flew with dead and wounded aboard. He baled himself out of fatal spins, where the G-force could suck your insides out. Then one day he was chatting to one of the other pilots, a mate of his, lad from Northampton, queer as a coot apparently, and as he was talking to him he saw his face turn into a skull.

**Rosie** You're making this up!

**George** And this lad, the gayboy, went out on a raid on the Ruhr that night and got himself shot down and killed. And then my dad started seeing it all the time. The skull lurking beneath the face. And every time he saw it in a lad's face he knew the boy wouldn't make it. He could tell from just looking at their faces. In the end they kicked him out, said he couldn't fly any more, he was gutted . . . LMF. Lack of Moral Fibre. Bastards.

*George goes up to Felix. He grabs hold of his face and pulls it closer to him, looks at him.*

**Rosie** Dad, stop it right now. You're drunk. Go on. Go away.

**George** No. Just what I thought. (*George lets go of his face dismissively and walks out. Pause.*)

**Rosie** He's harmless really.

**Felix** Mmm.

*Pause.*

**Felix** Rosie –

**Rosie** No, that subject is vetoed.

*Pause.*

**Felix** My father once said that a beehive was the blueprint for a Utopia in which the sexual impulse would cease to exist. He must have been going through a difficult time when he said it . . . But I don't think he was right. I think a hive is a blueprint for a world in which the men are totally useless. The women do all the work and the men, once they've fertilised the women, the men, well . . . die.

**Rosie** Seems like a good system to me.

**Felix** Clearly.

*like Ophelia*

**Rosie** Felix. What did you expect me to do after you left me? Hie myself to a nunnery?

**Felix** I think you should have told me.

**Rosie** You didn't deserve to know.

**Felix** You used to be straight with me.

**Rosie** Well, things aren't black and white for me any more. That's what it's like to be a parent. Anyway, I don't care what you think of me. I brought up my daughter on my own. She is a credit to me. I am a good person.

**Felix** I know that.

**Rosie** Good.

**Felix** Why did you want to have sex with me again?

**Rosie** I don't know. It wasn't just a casual fuck, if that's what you mean. Nothing with you is ever casual, Felix.

**Felix** I tried to imagine what it would be like if we were together again –

**Rosie** Don't waste your time. I wouldn't have you.

**Felix** No. Good call.

*After a pause they both smile. Rosie looks at her watch.*

**Rosie** I've got to go and collect her. She gets anxious if I'm late.

**Felix** Did you really name her after me? happiness?

*Pause. Rosie shrugs.*

I tried to picture it, you know, the last four weeks, introducing myself to her. I don't even know what a seven-year-old looks like.

**Rosie** She doesn't have your eyes, if that's what you're asking. She's her own little person.

**Felix** That wasn't what I meant.

**Rosie** She's about this high. Her face is full of freckles from the sun. She's just lost her front tooth. And her knees are covered in scabs. She's the most gorgeous child you'll ever see.

**Felix** I bet she is. (*Felix smiles. Pause.*)

**Rosie** She wants to know who her father is. She wants to know his story. This is for her, you know, not for me.

*Felix goes to speak.*

She is the best thing, Felix. I started writing a diary the day she was born – to record all the important moments, you know. The first time she spoke, caught a ball properly, tied her own shoelaces, rode a bicycle without stabilisers. I know it might sound dull from where you are standing –

**Felix** No, no, it doesn't. Eureka moments.

**Rosie** Yes, that's nice. My life is full of Eureka moments now I have her.

**Felix** Yes.

**Rosie** I would like you to meet each other.

**Felix** What?

**Rosie** She would like you –

**Felix** No –

**Rosie** She wouldn't show it for a bit, you'd have to put a bit of work in, but she's so thirsty for knowledge, for answers, for how the world works –

**Felix** (*quietly*) I don't know how the world works.

**Rosie** I mean things like all the names of the stars, the constellations –

**Felix** You can get a b–book for that.

**Rosie** A book isn't the same.

**Felix** Rosie. I would be next to useless.

**Rosie** Well, that's not as bad as completely useless.

**Felix** It's worse than useless. At least with useless you know where you are.

**Rosie** No you wouldn't be.

**Felix** Rosie. I can't do this . . . I'm sorry. I'd like to give you some money, though –

**Rosie** Oh, shut up, Felix. You have spent too much of your life theorising. Don't you realise how brilliant this offer is, how generous I am being? I am offering you a chance to be. Just to be.

**Felix** It's too late.

**Rosie** Of course it's not. She is a child! If she is up for having a dad after seven years of being without one, then you bloody well should be. (*Rosie goes up to him. She embraces him, kisses his head.*) It's probably the best offer that you will ever ever get.

*He nods. She goes. Felix stays where he is.*

**Felix** (*quietly, rehearsing it, clumsily, unconvinced by his performance*) Felicity. Felicity. This is Cassiopeia and Andromeda and that is Pegasus and Ursa Major of course, and . . . erm . . . Ursa Minor –

*Flora enters.*

**Flora** Talking to yourself? Where's George?

**Felix** I don't know.

86

**Flora** Has Rosie gone?

**Felix** Yes.

**Flora** Oh. Right. Mercy's calmed down, thankfully.

**Felix** I'm going today, Mother.

**Flora** I see.

**Felix** I'll have to get my things in order. (*Felix puts the ashes down. He takes a letter out of his pocket. He hands it to his mother.*)

**Flora** What's this?

**Felix** It came today. I wanted to give it to you earlier b–but there wasn't a right moment.

**Flora** It's addressed to your father.

**Felix** Yes. I opened it, I hope you don't mind.

**Flora** What is it?

**Felix** It's from the Royal Entomological Society.

**Flora** Oh. I'll look at it later.

**Felix** No, look at it now.

*Flora opens the letter. She reads it. He watches her. She folds it up and puts it away.*

You were wrong about him. He did make his mark. In his own small way. (*He goes to go.*) Oh, and Mother, you know you told me about the day you took me to prep school and how you waved and waved to me until I was a b–black dot. Until after I was a black dot . . . The thing that you've forgotten, Ma, is that I didn't look b–back. I never looked back.

*Perhaps he goes to get the ashes and then changes his mind. He exits, leaving the ashes behind him. Flora watches him.*

**Flora**  Felix?

*He does not turn round. She is left on her own. She picks up the ashes gingerly and holds them to her for a moment. George enters.*

**George**  There you are, bun. I've been looking for you.

*She puts the ashes down carefully on the steps to the hive. He watches her.*
   *She is distracted.*

**George**  What is it, bun? What's happened?

**Flora**  James discovered a new species of bumblebee before he died.

**George**  What?

**Flora**  An official letter came.

**George**  That's good.

**Flora**  It's such a shame that it arrived late. That he never read it. The recognition.

**George**  Yes.

**Flora**  It's something he always wanted to do – to find and name a new species. He said it was the best way to make your name as a bee-keeper. The only way to have your name live on after death.

**George**  Good for James.

**Flora**  It's a variety of the small garden bumblebee, *Bombus hortorum*, only the queen is smaller and more delicately built.

**George**  (*humouring her*) Is she?

**Flora**  But the point is, he didn't name it after himself, you see. He named it after me. *Bombus floratum.* Flora's Bumblebee.

**George** Well, that's nice of him. I bet she's a looker.

**Flora** I can't marry you.

**George** Bun –

**Flora** I'm very, very sorry.

**George** What are you saying?

**Flora** It's not right.

**George** Bollocks.

**Flora** Our families hate each other.

**George** Our families can go to hell.

**Flora** And I am already married.

**George** No, well, we'll live in sin. Bugger it.

**Flora** No, George.

**George** You said James wasn't enough for you. You said –

**Flora** He wasn't. But neither are you. I'm sorry. I am a deeply ungrateful woman, I always want more and it is my undoing, you see.

**George** I'll be more. I'm only just getting into my stride.

**Flora** It doesn't feel right. Being here in this garden. With you. Since James died nothing has felt right.

**George** We'll move. We'll get somewhere else.

**Flora** Don't you see that it only worked when there were three of us? Everything had a place. And now there is no equilibrium.

**George** You're just disorientated. You're feeling guilty.

**Flora** Yes.

**George** I understand.

**Flora** No, you don't. I feel like I've lived my whole life in miniature. And I am not a miniaturist. I have tried my hardest to break out but I cannot.

**George** We can, we will . . . When Mary died I couldn't function –

**Flora** Yes. Poor Mary. Poor Mary, George.

**George** Yes, God love her, she went through it, she didn't deserve it but my life with her was humdrum, Flora. Charming but humdrum. But when I think about you . . . I fee . . . like –

**Flora** (*interrupting*) Oh spare me the metaphor. At our age it's all such a cliché.

**George** Why? Why should it be? What do you want?

**Flora** I don't want. To want things has always been my gravest error. I am going to stifle it.

**George** Rubbish –

**Flora** George. I am so old. Not even the royal jelly will save me.

**George** You are beautiful –

**Flora** Beauty is not enough. It is never enough. Nature's cruel trick. When I was little I always thought that I was marked out, special, that I was on the verge of something momentous happening. I used to tingle with anticipation, I had legions of butterflies in my stomach. No that's not right. A flutter of butterflies, is it?

**George** What?

**Flora** James was very good with words. Knowing the right words.

**George** Please don't compare us. You said you never would.

**Flora** No, and I don't because it is impossible. You pale in each other's comparison. (*laughing*) Oh you, you George, you are a monumental man. When all this nonsense began I would be at the sink and the thought of you would catch me in my throat, wrap around me, flay me . . . You lack – precision that is all. But it doesn't matter.

**George** It does matter. I will change. I will be what you want me to be.

**Flora** It's too late. It has gone sour.

**George** No, it hasn't. You're just upset. Today has been –

**Flora** I am not upset. I am in a state of terminal disappointment.

**George** Please, Flora. Don't do this. I beg you. I can't cope with this. Everything will come right, I promise you. (*George is practically on his knees.*)

**Flora** (*hard*) We've been fooling ourselves, George.

**George** I haven't.

**Flora** We're just going through the motions.

**George** I'm not.

**Flora** It's all so vulgar. The whole bloody lot of it.

**George** No. I love you, please, bunny. Bunny girl.

*Felix enters. He is wearing the cricket whites that he was wearing in the first scene. He interrupts them. He is embarrassed.*

**Felix** I'm sorry. I didn't mean to – I was just getting my things together. I needed to – I forgot the –

**Flora** They're over there.

*Flora points at the ashes. Felix goes to get them.*

Will you be able to get a train at this time?

**Felix** I thought I might take the car, if that's all right?

**Flora** Fine.

*George starts to laugh uncontrollably.*

**George** Owzat!

**Felix** What?

**George** There he is. He's done it. He's won the bloody ashes.

**Felix** I'm going now.

**George** (*sourly*) Yes! You go. You've done your worst, now you bugger off.

**Flora** George.

**George** I'll tell you something for nothing. I'm glad you're not my son.

*Felix puts the ashes back down on the steps to the hive.*

**Flora** This is not Felix's fault.

**George** You bastard. You big fat lazy bumbling bastard.

**Flora** (*to Felix*) George and I have separated.

**George** Do you feel happy now? Now you've fucked everyone's life up?

**Felix** No.

**George** Perhaps Rosie was right. We're not good enough for the Humbles. We don't live up to their elevated standards.

**Flora** That is not true.

**George** And here he is, the highest flier of them all. Felix Humble. You want to be careful, you could be heading for a fall. You know what happened to Icarus, don't you? Oh sorry, did I shock you all there with a literary allusion? I do beg your pardon, getting above my station.

**Flora** George –

**George** Well, Icarus and his dad, I can't remember his name but he was a boring old fart whoever he was, he probably kept bees in his spare time, well they decided they'd go for a little fly, like you do, so they made their wings of wax – ah! wax, see, from the buggering bees he kept on the side –

**Flora** I think we're familiar with the story.

**George** Don't interrupt me, Flora, not when I'm at full throttle. So they made their wings of wax and feathers and shit and then Icarus, Icky to his mates, not that he had many, Icky flew slap bang into the sun, like the stupid twat that he was.

**Flora** George –

**George** So my advice to you, Humble boy, is head for the skies. Yes, do us all a favour and keep following that star.

**Flora** I think you should go.

**George** You're a beautiful woman, Flora, but your problem is you disappeared up your own arse some time ago. You want to wake up and smell the roses. Oh dear, sorry, *faux pas*.

*Felix goes up to him, takes him by the arm.*

**Felix** You've said your b–b–bit.

**George** Good, wasn't it? I thought I put it quite well. (*George shakes Felix off roughly.*) I'm going, I'm going.

*George starts to walk away. He is calm but just before he exits he picks up a hoe from the back wall where all the garden equipment is kept. He swings round and charges at Felix. Felix at first defends himself with the gardening stool. The fight continues around the garden, over the table, round the hammock. Various garden implements get used: the trowel, the garden fork, a pair of secateurs. Perhaps at one point Flora picks up the small water sprayer and sprays George with it. The dialogue continues through the fight.*

Right. Let's be having you, you bastard.

**Flora** George, stop it, stop it right now.

**George** Let's see how light he is on his feet.

**Felix** Please stop. I don't want this –

**George** Not bad for a lardy. Come on, run, come on Icky, let's see you fly.

**Flora** George, this is ridiculous.

*Suddenly Felix turns round and attacks him back. George starts to overpower him.*
*Felix suddenly stops. He is breathless.*

**Felix** Don't hurt me.

**George** I knew you didn't have it in you.

**Felix** No, you're right. I don't.

*George approaches him.*

**Flora** Oh no, please don't hurt him.

*But suddenly George stops as well.*

**George** What the –?

*He is swatting his hands around him in a demented fashion. At the same time as he does this Jim the gardener comes on. Felix sees him, but Flora and George do not look at him. George is swatting away a bee that is attacking him.*

**George** Get off me, you little bastard. I thought you got rid of them. Get off. (*He continues to swat the bee away and move from spot to spot to try and get rid of the bee.*)

**Felix** (*looking at Jim*) They're back.

**George** Do something, Flora.

**Felix** The bees are back.

**George** Get a spray, for Christ's sake.

**Felix** Let there be b–bees!

**Flora** You mustn't fight it.

**George** It's bloody mental.

**Flora** Don't threaten it.

**George** It's trying to bloody kill me.

**Flora** Well then, go! I've told you a hundred times to go.

**George** Jesus Christ!

*George makes a very inelegant exit. He is still pursued by the bee. Flora still has her back to Jim.*

**Jim** Exit pursued by a bee. The ghost

*Flora reacts strangely to Jim's voice. She doesn't turn round.*

**Flora** What?

**Jim** That was the queen. Lovely little thing, but don't rile her!

**Flora** Oh my God.

**Felix** You can hear him? Mother! Please tell me you can hear him.

*Flora nods.*

**Jim** She's probably the only one left now. The others will have dropped out of the sky.

**Flora** A finite number of wingbeats.

**Jim** That's right.

**Felix** Turn around, Mother. Look at him.

**Flora** He's here?

**Felix** All summer he has been here with me. In the garden.

**Flora** Oh my God.

**Felix** Like pointing a telescope at a blank bit of the sky and seeing a star that I have never seen before.

*She turns around slowly. She looks at him. Slowly there is music.*

**Flora** James.

**Felix** You can see him?

**Jim** *Bombus floratum.*

**Flora** Yes!

**Jim** Flora's Bumblebee. Do you like her?

**Flora** I do.

**Felix** All summer he has been with me. But I didn't know what to say.

**Jim** Flora.

**Flora** (*to James*) The first time I saw you, I knew.

**Jim** Yes.

**Flora** I knew that no one would ever look at me like this again.

*Their speech overlaps slightly as they feed each other with the lines.*

**Jim** Outside the exam halls –

**Flora** – of the School of Biology –

**Jim** – I had been writing about flowers –

**Flora** – the pollination of flowers –

**Jim** – and I saw you. The sun is shining around your head –

**Flora** – and you come towards me – your gown flapping in the wind –

**Jim** – like I'm flying towards you –

**Flora** – and you look at me –

**Jim** – I look at you –

**Flora** – and you say –

**Jim** Did you drop from the sky?

*Pause.*

**Felix** (*quietly*) Eureka.

*Felix looks at both of them. They are transfixed with each other. They come together.*

**Jim** My Flora.

**Flora** James Humble. Bachelor of Science.

*Felix is apart from them.*
*He stumbles off.*

**Flora** James, I'm sorry – I'm so sorry –

**Jim** (*to Flora*) Hush. I have to tell you about the flowers – all the flowers I have planned for you . . .

**Flora** Yes. Tell me the names. The names of all the flowers.

*As Jim lists the flowers, Flora slowly starts to cry.*

**Jim** *Papaver dubium.*

**Flora** A poppy?

**Jim** Doubtful poppy. To help you sleep. *Dianthus barbatus.* Sweet William. For peace.

**Flora** Yes.

**Jim** *Mimosa sensitiva.* For scent. *Zinnia elegans.* Elegant like my Flora.

**Flora** A sunflower, I'd like a sunflower.

**Jim** *Helianthus multiflorus.*

**Flora** And some love-in-a-mist.

**Jim** Whatever you want.

**Flora** Some love-lies-a-bleeding.

**Jim** *Amaranthus procumbens.*

**Flora** Some St John's wort –

**Jim** *Hypericum perforatum* – for sadness. *Lythrum salicaria* – purple loosestrife, for contentment. *Oenothera biennis* – evening primrose, for ease of heart.

**Flora** Some bluebells.

**Jim** *Campanula rotundifolia.* For the spring.

**Flora** And more scented flowers. I need more scent. I need to be able to smell them again.

**Jim** *Lavandula spica.* Blue and white varieties. *Passiflora caerulea.* Passion flowers. *Dianthus deltoides. Syringa vulgaris.* Some sweet-scented heliotrope. Clematis and honeysuckle. My bees love that. Buddleia for the butterflies. Scented hyacinths. French marigolds. *Tagetes Patula. Aster multiflorus. Amaryllis aurea.* Can you smell them all?

**Flora** Yes. Yes, I can. I think I can.

**Jim** Good. (*He goes to go.*)

**Flora** No, please, James. Please don't go.

**Jim** All the bees have gone now. It's only the queen left. *Bombus floratum.* She'll have to do the winter on her own, but she'll manage that. She's strong.

**Flora** No. No, I can't.

*He leads her to the rose bush. He bends down and smells it. He gestures that she should do the same. She does so. She breathes deeply, takes in the scent.*

**Jim** There.

**Flora** Yes.

*He exits. As he does, the hive lights up, and then fades. She looks up.*
  *The music changes suddenly to a humming, resonant of bees and a revving car engine. Flora reacts as if she had tinnitus in her ear.*

**Flora** I can't do the winter on my own. Felix. Felix? Oh my God. Please God – Felix!

*She runs towards the exit. Felix appears.*

**Flora** I thought you'd gone – I thought you'd –

**Felix** I was just starting up the car.

**Flora** Suddenly I had this terrible feeling you'd . . .
I don't know what I thought. It was stupid of me.

**Felix** No, no, it wasn't stupid. At the beginning of the
summer I thought I was going to – But I'm not brave
enough to let go.

**Flora** Thank God!.

**Felix** B–b–but I just want . . . the p–possibility . . . of
another life, Ma.

*Pause. Felix picks up the ashes.*

**Flora** Say the words. You know them. You've always
known them.

**Felix** (*with difficulty*) The night we watched the moon-
landings together, Dad cried. And in that moment, he
made me want to fly. He held my hand and he gave me
the courage to defy physics and fly anyway. The day that
a man landed on the moon Dad cried. And the day he
died the sun cried bees. The sun cried bees. (*He takes the
lid off the pot.*) I release my father to space. To the
limitless quiet of space. To fly in unending silence.
Through a black hole. Past the event horizon. To the
state of singularity. Dust to immortal dust. And out and
on and beyond. To a new universe. A parallel world.

**Flora** A better place.

**Felix** The land of milk and honey.

*Felix scatters the ashes. They watch them settle in
silence.*

There.

**Flora** Yes.

*An awkward moment between them.*

Will you still be going back –?

**Felix** In a little while.

**Flora** It's getting dark, maybe you should set off in the morning, when it's light. And you've eaten next to nothing –

**Felix** (*a hint of irritation*) Mother.

*Flora looks at Felix, perhaps she touches him lightly but unsentimentally.*

**Flora** Well. (*She goes to go in.*) Don't expect me to wave you off.

*He smiles. The sound of a bee humming somewhere in the distance.*

**Felix** Let b–b–b–be.

*Flora smiles and exits. He is left alone in the garden in the failing light. Felix pauses, swallows and smiles.*

Let be.

*Lights fade.*